Little Minutes

STEVEN PROP

ISBN: 979-8-89419-566-7 (sc)
ISBN: 979-8-89419-567-4 (hc)
ISBN: 979-8-89419-568-1 (e)

THE EWINGS PUBLISHING

One Galleria Blvd., Suite 1900, Metairie, LA 70001
(504) 702-6708

Dedication

This book is dedicated to the memories of
Mark Johns of Fairbanks, Alaska,

And

John Phillips of Munhall, Pennsylvania.

Forward

This is what I do
when I have the energy
and I remember to do it.

These are the battles I fight
when I have the strength to fight them.

These are the songs I write
when I can convince myself to write them.

When I can convince myself that they are worthy placeholders,
while I bide my time riding the dirty needle
Into that fat groove in the vinyl,
becoming one with the static……..

Contents

Getting Warmed Up

About Mark

Albatross and Tumbleweed

Introducing The Unquiet Mind

And now for something sure to make you scratch your head and say, Huh?

Fun with Haiku!

And Now For More Of The Completely Expected

Getting Warmed Up

Existentially Challenged: Am I Here? Am I Not? Is That Bacon I Smell?

I walk among you.
Unseen.
Inaudible,
Nonexistent.

I was speaking.
I was in midsentence
when a friend I'd known for years
cut me off.
The other three,
also, people I had known for years,
slowly looked from me to her.
I protested but no one heard me.
I touched them, I grabbed hands.
No one felt my presence.
I decided to play their game.
(Was it a game?)

I decided to become invisible.
All I had to do was close my mouth.
You can't imagine the thrill of watching
one person after another
look right through you.
And the liberation you gain
when you're not loud enough
or there enough
for anyone to care.
For anyone to see you.

2

You just fade into the background.
You morph.
You become the patina that forms on the wall.
In plain sight.

You are the thing,
unseen.
The thing that holds the wall up.
The dirty, gritty patina.
The world would stop moving
without you.
But no one takes any notice of you
until you're not there
to not be seen.

Your presence doesn't matter,
doesn't register,
until the walls fall down.
Then they may miss you.
The scapegoat must be found.

I have become invisible.
I am useful only in that
I am useless.
The beautiful loser.
The blade sharp,
but not sexy.
The serviceable
Undesired.

The dog under the porch,
treated well only out of a sense

3

of obligation.
Thank God for obligation.
Thank God for the porch.
Hang the master.

I am the walker looking for eye contact
to avoid.
I never have to turn my head away.
Transparency,
the gift that keeps on giving.

Small talk only happens in the space
between my ears.
Isolation from fellow travelers
got me dancing tween the tears.
Alienation from the mob enforcing
all my fears.
That inner voice so sinister
condemning me
for all my wasted years.

I am the tree.
Come,
hide with me,
or behind me.
Breathe slow.
Remain silent and
watch the world with me
as we escape its attention,
in this present.
In this state of transparency
and unavailing existence.

Paranoid? Maybe

Make way for the moral stragglers.
Make way for the critical eye.
Make way for a last stand,
a frantic, desperate lunge
with intent to grasp.
Make way for your fleeing integrity.
Make way for the traditions that have been
beaten into you.
They too are part of this exodus.

Make way for an Armani suit and
A flag lapel,
spewing its virtue
and sliding a hand under
your daughter's dress.

Make way for all the virtue signalers.
The dividers.
The useful idiots.
The drummer boys,
and buglers.
Their battle cry is righteous,
and flexible.

Faced with loss,
they convert.

Embrace the haste,
your first impressions
are straight and narrow.

Your execution is true.
The execution of you,
It will be claimed to have never happened,
or,
You were the enemy.

The criminal.
The adversary.
And you got exactly what you deserved.
Because you didn't think
what we told you to.

Kicking and Screaming

The past has been speaking to me,
in hushed tones,
through snapshots
and memories.

Father Time reminds me of how
arrogant a young man can be.
The whipping post is mine.
"You earned it" he says.

Pick your poison well.
We are not nearly as cavalier in
our waning hours
as we were when the days were long
and our reason was short.

When we could run all day,
drink and fornicate all night,
and fatigue was only a rumor.

Tight skin and definition were entitlements.
And only in commissioned caricatures
would bags be found under our eyes.

The calendar
and the mirror
are now my enemies.
My people are the collateral damage
in the war being waged upon me.

It's not a price I want to pay.
What is your poison?
Does it define you?
Listen to and watch your reflection.
Does it malign you?
Wade through those memories.
What are the feelings
that they assign to you.

Stress fractures in the gray matter.
I'm jumping for branches,
I'll never reach.

On the way down
I look down.

My clothes are dirty
and my bones are weary with ache.

I do not own a white flag.
I cannot beat father time.

But,
I will not lose gracefully.
I will enact a scorched earth campaign,
and I will employ it,
hastily.

Blue Hour Tumbleweed

The blue hour cuts through your lonely heart,
filleting the soul that has nothing to cling to.
The war that it wages,
in bitter waves and stages
is all to evident on your face as it ages.
The blue hour is on the field.
And You are the rolling transient.
Rolling through wheat and desert.
Nothing to cling to.
Nothing clinging to you.
No anchor to hold you.
No master to scold you.
No sculptor to mold you.
You left your point of origin
and never bothered to stake another claim.
The blue hour isn't a place, but you live there.
And you hold it
like a piece of hallowed ground.
You chase it as the world spins around.
Screaming your war cry, never making a sound.
You are a slave to the wind as the earth continues to spin.
The elements tear you down.
In the Blue hours you confront your sins.
You count them off.
One at a time.

But you never stop moving.
You are always willing to toe the line.
You never assess your opponents.
You've never bothered to see,
an adversary's strength,
their intellect
or their pedigree.
By luck alone you've made it this far down the line.
Kicking around in strange pastures,
and competing in your mail in chess game with Father Time.

Athena Stands Mighty

Half-naked and in the corner.
She will not look down.
Her chin is up, as is her resolve.
She meets your slings and arrows,
mournfully.
Because she needs to be wanted.
Deftly,
because she is not helpless.
And savagely,
because you underestimated her,
and she will not suffer under the weight of your ignorance.
Is there anything more beautiful than a
woman who knows her worth,
a woman who refuses to look down.
Conviction, thy name is Athena.

Indifference, the Lie

Bitter is the taste of absence.
It is neglect by alternative means.
I'm changed by the weight of
your truancy.
I'm haunted by my isolation,
unforeseen.

Never will I expose my desire.
Never will you hear me invite.
Never will I look up at you from
dirty knees.
I will not take what I crave
out of spite.

Pride has made me unyielding.
I tell the world I need nothing
it has.
But you are the bait the world
is wielding.
My resolve diminishes
by halves.

The entire Goddamn world
is between us.
Only are we acquainted by our
words.
I keep yours like lightning
in a bottle.
Precious,
fatal,
written
and unheard.

I long for a day I can touch you,
feel your skin under mine.
I want to taste the air around you.
On your quintessence my eyes
must dine.

But for now
I am deprived of your being.
My depravity, hyper-aware.
I'm an animal
avoiding capture and confinement.
I'm a beast with nary a care.

I'm a child
dancing between snares.

Blood Tunnel

These days
there are no crowded hours.
Just quiet
dark
abandon corners where one can
hear a pulse.

Sometimes that's a blessing,
sometimes a curse.

Run through the blood tunnel.

Should you reach for the random stranger?
Feed them your grief, choke them with it?
Fill that glass.
Neat.
With no garnish.
Pull the head back by the hair and
pour that wet, rusty failure
you've been brewing
onto a stoney face,
with ungiving eyes
and an unopened, unsullied mouth.

Run through the blood tunnel.

Or should you jump from
shadow to shadow,
trailing the crowd,

waiting
for the opportunity to present
an irradiant silhouette,
to say brilliant things,
to make shock and awe your calling card.
Busking
with no violin.
No accordion.
No guitar or harmonica.
Trading in wit and beauty for a few
fleeting moments,
little minutes
of evaporating connection to those that are
similarly broken,
but not alone.

Run through the blood tunnel.

Find your crowded hours and
collect them.
You were built to make more noise
than a pulse in a quiet,
dark corner.
Open your eyes and
lift your face toward Heaven.
Laugh loud
as you run through
the blood tunnel.

About Mark

The Anomaly

He never takes things too seriously.
He would rather laugh than cry.
Even in anger,
he would never speak imperiously.
And for him, "Hello" isn't nearly as easy
as "Goodbye".

Sweetly is the way he slays you.
Candor drips from his lips like nectar.
He sings you praises as he fillets you,
interpreting your tickertape favorably
in the presence of would-be objectors.

He'll lend a hand
If and when you need it.
But laughs heartily when you step in shit.
He's not your sweetest nor your best friend.
And he's happy in the mud
while slinging it.

Got a dirty job that needs doing?
Leave the angels at home.
Grab this soft spoken thesaurus
of modern slang
and a couple of blunt objects.
He'd never let you get dirty alone.

Broken Things

Oh my.
Broken things.
Broken things have evolving souls,
And shiny lures.
They surge.
They bloom.
Broken things may leave you laughing
but they don't always say goodbye.
Broken things spend their time
attempting to unbreak the nearly
unsalvageable,
while they recoil from their own
reflection.
Broken things laugh and
smile in the crowd.
Nary a care in the world.
As helpful as the day is long.
Broken things
pull the shades when
they're alone.
They make peace
with the darkness.
They make peace
with the noiseless, voiceless,
sequestered void.
A destination that must be warmed up to.
A destination that grows on a soul.

Broken things don't always say goodbye.
Broken things aren't
always recognizable
as broken.
And they don't always let you in.
They speak to you of shared experience.
In nostalgic tones,
with far away eyes
and delightful, slightly sad smiles.
Broken things warm you
From the inside out.
And they break your heart,
have no doubt.
Broken things don't always say goodbye.
Oh my.
How could we not see?
I didn't know you were broken.

The Anomaly II

In my mind you are significant.
You always cast a shadow
in the circles we ran in
and the circles that ran us.

I can't imagine the colors that would be missing
in my life,
were you never.

A field without wildflowers,
without clover,
were you never.

Bacon without eggs,
a joke without a punchline,
were you never.

A hook without bait,
A knife without an edge,
were you never.

Food with no flavor,
and words with no soul,
were you never.

Were you never you
would music sound the same?
Would I ever have given a damn,
would I still play this game?

Would life have been as cheerless
as life seems to be right now,
Were you never?

Were you never you,
Would she be her
and he be him,
and I be me?
Were you never,
would they be they
or we be we?

Were you never?
Were you just a character in a book?
The lovable antihero?
Backyard mechanics the world over,
would they still recognize you as their
fearless leader,
were you never in my circle?

Well, I know you were,
and you are.
And there is a legacy,
and a legend,
and lessons,
and soul.
You may be gone my friend,
but I have color and wildflowers
and clover.

You were.
I know.
We know,
and you will live forever.
Haunting and solid,
just below the surface,
like permafrost.

1-907-37X-XXXX

I nearly dialed your number
in the hopes that they were wrong.
They were not.
And now all I can think is,
there is no light in the Golden Heart City.
Tonight, the Northern Lights
will not shine.
The 907 has lost its color,
its flavor.
It is charmless,
pallid,
and inhospitable.
Where did you go?
Why?

Collateral Damage On A Long Slow Fuse

The Unquiet Mind:

"Hey *boy*. You haven't had much to say lately."
"Something on your mind?"
"Did you lose something this week?"
"Did you lose someone this week?"
"Did you lose some time, *boy*?"
"Did you think there was plenty of it?"

"It had only been twenty-two years. Why wouldn't you think you'd meet again? Grab those fishing rods and head down to the river; pack a bowl, grab a six pack and run around town in that big-ass box body chevy. Weren't the two of you cool?"

"Hey *boy*. Does it hurt?"

"Do you just wanna look straight up and scream? How does it feel to know that he turned out his own lights? Maybe he's better than you. How does it feel to know that he didn't reach out with his intent? To you. To anyone. He saw hopelessness, no path forward. Is that what it was *boy*? You don't even know, do you? A significant part of your life, a significant part of your time. One of the people who shaped what you became, and now he's probably going to end up in a jar. Never reached out, never cried for help. It wasn't his style. Approaching the end like he did everything else, face forward and unflinching. Another vet, checking out."

"When you gonna check out *boy*? Aren't you tired of me whispering in your ear, like a breeze through the wheatfield? Soft and inviting. Look at how the stalks sway, they dance. They invite. They hypnotize. Mother Nature is looking to recycle you, *boy*. Your friend answered the call. What's wrong with you?"

"Don't you want to dance with the casualties of autumn?"

"Well, I'm still here waiting for you *boy*. Every time you stub your toe, every time your heart breaks, anytime you want to step up and hand me your ticket. Unlike you, I've got all the time in the world, I'm patient. I'm here to punch it for ya, *boy*."

Me: "Hey"
Unquiet mind: "Yeah *Boy*?"
Me: "Fuck off!"

Mark Johns

Movement.

I'm anxious to see the grace in the circles you travel.
I'm a fan of movement and
the influence you wield.
The circles you move,
wherever you move them.
The minds that you change,
wherever you change them.
The hearts that you mend,
wherever you mend them.
The wars that you wage,
wherever you wage them.
The plays that you stage,
wherever you stage them.
The lives that you save,
wherever you save them.
I am a fan of movement.
Wherever you are,
you move me.
Restricted movement,
boundaries?
Not for you.
You must move the world and
I must love you for it.

Albatross and
Tumbleweed

Fate and the Flight of the Albatross

I knew the ancient mariner.
I'm a traveler far and wide.
I use the clouds for cover round the sundogs where I ride.
I ride the currents effortlessly.
I'm master of wind and sky.
I'm a lonely hunter; lonesome but not shy.
Six years on the wind.
Rarely touching ground.
Now I return to the point of my origin,
where camaraderie may be found.
And on the ground at last with a generation of my peers,
I set about my business,
No hesitation, apprehension, or fear.
The business of finding a partner,
a lover,
a friend.
We'll sail them skies together forever,
joined until the end.
And if the end comes fast
and I hit the briny sea,
leave my carcass to the sharks,
but raise a glass for me.
My spirit will never leave you.
I will follow you to your end.
I will wait for you on the other side.
Your phantom.
Your lover.
Your friend.

Melissa the Empath

Hypnotic.
She wields the power
of suggestion
through a glance.
Like your Mama did with a word.
You are no more likely
to evade her will
then you are to escape
this world unchanged.

She will punch you in the soul.
From your knees
you will beg her
to do it again.
And she must!
She is your empath.
Your seeress.

You are her garden.
You feel the scythe
when she swings it,
but she is the one that bleeds.

She feeds you with blood
on soil.
She feeds you with the light
in her eyes.

You have no choice but to grow
because she is the Sower,
divinely assigned to you.
Without her,
you're just another weed.

Take It

I didn't tell you what I wanted
because I was afraid
you wouldn't let me have it.

Imagine the surprise I experienced
when you walked right over to me
and took what I wanted to give you,
without my having said a word.

I am ready to give you more.
Maybe,
surrender is a better word.
Take it.
You are the harvester.
I am the crop.
Take it.
I will feed you for a season.
You will feed on my will.
Take it.
Your hands and heart were built for larceny,
your mouth for sin and blasphemy.
Take it.
My resolve.
My love.
Take it.

You better hope these are quality restraints,
or that you break me.
Because if I break these bonds
I'm going to take you.
And there is not a damn thing
you will be able to do about it.
Except to know your heart,
acknowledge your fate
and surrender.
I wonder, will you love being mine
as much as I love being yours?

Saccharine Aspirations

Here's to the things
that get lost.
Stolen by your busy day.
And you,
oblivious to the absence.

The thing you didn't say.
You meant to.
You swore you would remember.
But now, the sentiment is gone,
as is the perfect cadence,
as is the flawless abstraction.
Lost!
Stolen by distraction.

Here's to the things
that get lost.
Those perfect little dreams
you dream,
as you conduct the business
of someone who has managed
to make their own dream
your priority.

Their perfect little dreams
nurtured
in your perfect little hands
at the expense of your own
crystal,
saccharine aspirations.

Here's to the things
that get lost.
A coherent motivation for
the things that you do.

Introspection no longer
informs action.
They're just strange bedfellows
going through the motions.
So familiar,
one with the other.
So long together,
unlikely to part
despite the world between them.
Contemptible and lazy toward the other.
Yet terrified of a parting.

Here's to the things
that get lost,
during your busy day.
Your integrity.
Your resolve.
Your sense of justice
And empathy.

I Love that filtered lens through which
you see the world.
What color is yours?
Mine is green.
I would look in the mirror,
But I'm afraid of what I may
not see.

Here's to the things
that are lost.
Those saccharine aspirations.
Good riddance.
Trouble me no more.

Our Pages are Numbered.

There is status to be found
as a loner.
A position of power
she could never find in the group.
A piece of mind in being
one's own owner.
Never bound to the will
of the troop.

She trades in walk-away conversation,
a nod of her head
and a good deed or two.
With no noise
she assesses her situations
and she determines if she'll
play through.

She owns her success
as well as her failure,
both children she'll
nurture till the end.
She does it her way
by night and by day.
Brilliant,
the garden she tends.

Criminal indeed to yoke her.
She's worth more
than the team combined.
Foolish to have claimed
you broke her.
There is far
too much steel
in her spine.

She is the letter,
the word,
the pages.
The volume
speaking volumes with
merely a look.
She is the revelation,
the crescendo,
The last and most enlightening chapter.
Never
was she not the reason
for the writing of the entire book.

Her chapter.
Her gracious, thundering chapter.
All too brief.
So illuminating.

Same Destination. Different Roads.

I am a shadow
in the shadows,
a pebble in the sand,
a maple leaf on the lawn in autumn.
I'm a blade of grass
hiding on an acre
of land.

I am the faces in the crowd,
every color under the sun.
I'm thirty-two flavors of ice cream.
I'm the posse,
and the one who runs.

Easily are you beguiled
by a sneaky hand
and shiny things.
Susceptible to misdirection,
all too eager
to kiss the ring.

And you believe it when they say
they need you.
You're laid low when they say they don't.
You're in the clouds when
they say they'll use you,
and on the rails when
you find they won't.

40

You are the control specimen in a
petri dish,
the one right next to mine.
We are destined for the same fate,
not a minion,
mine is coming sooner.
and as you are on the inside,
yours will be slightly late.

But make no mistake my friend,
we are headed to the same summer camp.
Accept your tattoo with alacrity,
as I embrace my role as a tramp.

Ocean Enchanter

When you stand before the Atlantic
peering east.
When you recall the ancient words
that excite wonder
and bring down the walls.
When the horizon changes color.
When the sundogs bark and dance before you.
When you hear the distant aircraft
over London
and see only dragonflies.
When the tide walks back
your apprehensions.
When you are willing to put your hand forward
to grasp mine,
to clutch the formless,
to conjure me from the salt air.

Listen to the seaweed bubble.
Listen to the gulls and terns.
Feel the sun
tempered by the breeze.
Reach for what your heart does yearn.
I am the salt on the breeze.
I am the mist in the air.
I am the thorn on the rose
and I have the time to spare.

I will bring you low.
You can't count the tears we'll cry.
But I will paint your name on the mountain
as I teach your heart to fly.

Very few are only one thing.
You maybe ocean,
but you may also be sky.
You may be the rock
that life is bruised against.
I may be the bruised.
I may be the sand.
You may be the plow
or the lash.
Did you bring the sword or the sexton?
If you could only have one, which would you choose?
I will whisper in your ear.
I will tell you what to want.
You will feel my whiskers
as my lips release your lobe
and I resume my formless assault on your resolve,
and my incessant seeding
of your desire.

Because.
I am the salt on the breeze.
I am the mist in the air.
I am the thorn on the rose
and I have the time to spare.

I will build you up.
I will take you so very high.
I will paint your name on the mountain
as I teach your heart to fly.

On being Possessed

She's twisted with curves,
and the shutters cast shadows
on her alabaster flesh.

She's feeding my nerves.
Her shape is a road
I want to travel.
Every inch, a discovery.
Every destination from her toes
to her head,
a place to dine,
to discover,
to lay in wait.

She's feeding my mind as well.
She touched that place
inside of me,
the place that remembers,
the place that reaches out,
the place that separates the before her
and the after her,
then discards the before her.
She touched that place
from light years,
with the slightest of glances.

Her words are deployed
in a state of frugality.
I'm snared already.
She knows
that breath need not be wasted.
Verbosity is the equivalent of
pissing in the wind.

She never had to say a thing.
I am imprisoned between the shadows
that her shutters cast.
I will travel her twisted,
curving road.
I will explore her exotic,
undiscovered destinations.
I will write my name at the foot of her
ocean.

Baskets and Blankets

I could never love you
the way that you love me,
and it breaks my heart
every bit as much as it breaks yours.

You try to save face
and protest that love,
the love
that is written all over your face.
but every action you take
with regards to me
announces your heart's position
from the rooftops.

And you alert me
to the size of my own ego
for pointing out the snare
you've stepped in.
But,
since when is it
an act of monument building
to point out what one
shows the world?

And all I can do is watch,
and know
that I am the source
of your misery.

The anguish within you
beats like thunder on my ears
as your soul bleeds out
in a pool before me.

The exsanguination,
I could stop it temporarily.
I could lie to you.
is it better to destroy now,
or destroy you later?

I don't want to destroy you at all.
I just want to watch you
from the hill,
watch you in a field
of daisies and clover,
on your blanket
pulling soft white bread,
butter
and jam
from your wicker basket.
I want to watch you feed
your companions.
I want to see you lick away
that sweet, sticky jam from your lips
as you laugh with the joy
of a child.
And I cry with
the knowledge of the seasoned.

I could never give you that joy.
Grief is all I have
for the world.

Curse of the Tumbleweed

The prairie wind
is a lonely thing.
It makes a mournful sound.
It catches the dust and chafes your skin
while pushing tumbleweed around.

Tumbleweed cries for freedom while trapped against the
fence.
No expectation of emancipation. No promise of recompense.
And in his lucid yammering,
and through his struggle against the barbs,
he wears his contrition
for all to see,
it is his finest garb.
Praying for manumission,
importuning to roll free,
through his squeals he makes the deals
that gets him off his knees.

Released from the wall he was trapped against,
Tumbleweed again rolls free.
At the whim of the prairie wind,
indebted,
exhausted,
but free.

But what did he promise,
or bargain away
for a chance at life anew.
He had so vey little
to start with,
no family,
no home,
no view.

But Tumbleweed rolls
and pays the price,
and rolls a little more.
Assuring himself
all debts are paid
before he hits that door.
The door the prairie wind pushes him through.
The door that ends his journey.
Tumbleweed has nothing
to show for his life
but cracked skin and lines of worry.
So put down roots my dearest friends,
don't cast your lot with the wind.
You started your walk on this blue dot
with nothing and no one.
Don't end it with nothing and no one again.

I Have Never Known the World
Without Him In It

He's in that garden.
The garden where he loses himself.
He stands there like a statue,
reading his own history on grape leaves.
Quiet.
Unmoving.
The scarecrow, lost in thought.
He's only quiet
when He's on his own,
but never
not
lost in thought.
He built it all for others
as well as himself,
this magnificent garden.
He sent them invitations.
They did not come.

Bruised,
he shrugged his shoulders and
stood at the entrance
to his garden.
He hailed strangers,
hungry, or content.
He met them at the gate
with an embrace,
and a smile.
He fed them,

bellies and souls.
He raided the apiary
for the finest honey,
for them,
while they read their own histories
on his vines.
Never did it occur to him
to give too little.
Never had it occurred to him
that he had shared too much.
Never were they hungry or cold
in his presence.
Never lonely.
Never old.

His family came at a price
he could pay,
so he paid it.
This God of the apiary.
This scarecrow of the orchard.
This father in the garden.

He paid the price.
He never complained.
And when he grew weary
they raided the apiary,
and they brought him the comb.
His joy was sweet
and stuck to his lips.
Earned
with all the little minutes
and all the little sacrifices

and all the little victories.
With all the love he nurtured
and guarded like a treasure.
To his tribe,
he handed out hope
like pocket change.

To him his tribe
ascribed
the changing seasons,
renewal,
the promise of the coming day,
the voice that whispers to them
that they are the oak,
and that no mere catastrophe
can prevail against
an oak with the root structures
that they are endowed with.

The only thing that will take them,
that can take them,
that can take him
is time.
And when time took him
we didn't know whether to
laugh or cry.
So, we laid him in his garden
and read our histories on his grape leaves,
through tear drops
on smiling faces,
while his garden blooms brilliant
in perpetuum.

Fragmentation of Sanity in Real Time

Your soil is spent.
Not another pepper.
Not another Pea.
Your soul is bent,
twisted and anguished.
Kin to the willow tree.

North Dakota.
Your slender, gnarled finger points.
Sunflower season, passed in rain.
Secure the gifts of Autumn,
there's ibuprofen for the pain.
Face is haggard and unkept.
Not a handsome silhouette.
Habits, self-serving
and obscene.
Fingers stained with nicotine.

Anticipate the austerity of winter.
Tomatoes in jars.
Pickles in bars.
Drunks seeing stars.
Elon on Mars.
The future isn't ours.
Extension cords for cars.
Windshields under crowbars.
Lithium mining; bizarre,
when advocated by Earth Czars.

Fragmented.
Segmented.
Sentiment traded away.
Cult based on opinion.
The pride destroys the stray.
Fragments of thought.
Fragments of speech.
Fragments of character.
Fragmented compassion.
Fragmented joy.
Fragmented empathy.
Fragments.
Fragment.
Frag.
Fuck it!
Sometimes, it's all too much.

Reassignment of the Control Specimen

How broken are you?
How did you get it in your head
that you deserved to watch
as those you trusted
disassembled every part of you
that had felt something?

How did they convince you
to lay still and watch as
they picked you apart, piece by piece,
discarding your uniqueness
and then reassembling you,
incomplete?
Incomplete, but a carbon copy
of what they see when they look in the mirror.
Does it surprise you
when you open your mouth and
someone else's voice
booms forth
with someone else's creed?

Do you even remember who
you were when they told you that
you could be anything you put
your mind to
as long as your ambition exists
between lines they had drawn?
Did those lines ever extend beyond
a well-manicured lawn?

Have you ever felt the mud
between your toes?
Has anything ever surprised you?
Has anything ever taken your
breath away?

Have you ever turned around to see
just how infinitely long
the line you're standing in is?
Yet, life is short.
Find another line.
Find another voice.

Grab hope by the throat and convince her
to fuck the obsequiousness,
the cloying, obedient, pandering nature
right out of you.
You scarecrow, you decoy,
you empty, empty box.

When Youth and Passion Make Way
for the Pragmatic Passenger

He landed.
Ass over tea kettle,
several times.
He got up a little achy
but uninjured.
He shook the sand from
his body and plucked the
marsh grass from between
his feathers.

There was no grace about
him on the ground, but in the air,
riding the currents, he was a
ballet dancer with wings.
Fluid.
Lithe.
Sleek.

But, in the recent past
He has begun to feel time.
Feel it start to collect
the interest on the credit
it has extended him.

It was a little odd he thought
as he watched the sunset from
the beach.
Or Ironic.
In his mind, his days had gotten longer,
while the time he could devote to the
pursuit
and perfection of his endeavors
had grown shorter.
He could still perform.
He was still magnificent.
But, his plumage lacked it's
former luster,
and his routines, as impressive as they were,
were now also beautiful exercises
with an emphasis on brevity.

What happened to the Albatross that
with wings outstretched
could sleep among the stars?
Never did he worry about the space
between him and the ocean.

The albatross evolved
into something that
longs equally for
earth between webbed feet
as it does for air beneath wings.

And that albatross is willing to
take his chances
with the predators of the land
for now.
One day, he knows that his favorite place,
his sanctuary,
will evict him in a dramatic way.
It will cause him to become one with
the land, or ocean.
And when it does, he loathes the thought
that he may miss it
because his eyes were closed.

A Frozen Moment

Between heartbeats,
That's when the magic happened.
When I wasn't looking,
when I was busy doing everything
in my power not to notice....
You.

You cast your spell on the wind.
You opened your mouth and
it rolled off a velvet tongue
and took flight
on the breeze between us,
while I was occupied with things
that were not
You.
You.

I can never look at that street corner,
that storefront window,
or that yellow dress ever again
and not remember the long pause,
the big empty silence
between heartbeats.
The absence of movement in my chest
that lasted as long
as each of your easy strides.

Oh, how you walked with confidence.
Oh, your reflection in the window.

Oh, how your arms swung at your hips.
Oh, the shape and length of your legs.
Oh, that smile on your lips.

Your chin slightly raised,
and that smile.
For the gods?
For Savannah?
For the end of October?
Or just to torture me
from time to time
when I see that shade of yellow?

You are a witch.
I will hide in your autumn
and drink your cider
between heartbeats
and resolutions.
Bring the harvest. Bring the colors.
Bring the pralines and coffee.
Bring your heart.
Bring that smile,
and bring that magic that turns my head.

Bring me to the end
of the street
where the oaks
don their crowns of
Spanish moss
and take me from this world,
or tell my heart it's ok to beat without you.

Albatross and Tumbleweed

The Albatross and the Tumbleweed.
Will they ever have a meeting of the minds?
So much in common, so little to say.
Different roads to travel, similar games to play.
Both carried by the wind,
Forging paths of their own.
Headed for nirvana. They'll never call it home.
Tumbleweed rolls the plains, a drifter to the end.
Crossing fields in fallow. Avoiding foe and friend.
Albatross plies the treacherous skies with no place
to put his feet.
No feed. No meal. No youthful zeal. No friend or foe to meet.
Both searching for that thing.
That thing that makes them whole.
Coming up short day after day.
Failure eroding soul.

You Blinked

You left me in the street
I kept you from.

I suppose I had it coming.
"Hey Boy."

You told anybody that would listen
That I didn't take care of you.

There are those I failed.

You are not one of them.
"Hey boy."

You claim occupation of the moral high ground
And you look down at me from your perch.

So smug.
So satisfied.
So confident in your fabrications.
"Hey boy."

You never met a fairytale you didn't like,
as long as you didn't have to read it.

Effort. Effort is the dirtiest six letter word you know.
"Hey boy."

I know people who get up and fight a losing
battle every Goddamn day.
They know the deck is stacked against them.
And they come home every night with worn out knees
and grease under their nails
and a smile on their face.
You know why?

"Hey *Boy*."
Because someone behind that door is waiting for them.
Waiting in joy.

In the world I met you in you had nothing.

I kept you off the street you put me on.
"Hey *boy*."

You have everything you want.
All I wanted was you.
"Hey *Boy!*"

My character evaluator needs a tune up.

Truth's Silence Bondage

I fill the vacant spaces
with fiction.
I diminish the sharp edges
with friction.
I hand you my biography
with conviction.
I walk away,
embracing fully
the dereliction.

The One Who Leaves

The menu stares back at me like a college professor
waiting for an answer
she knows I do not have.
The waitress stands to my left.
I'm looking at the menu but waiting for you to order.
The waitress clears her throat.
I look up.
She asks me if I'm ready. I place an order.
She collects the menu; she looks at me oddly,
slowly turns
and walks to the kitchen.
There is a cup of coffee in front of me.
You have an iced tea. Beads of perspiration roll down the side,
the movement of which is louder than you.
My keys and wallet are off to the right
by the napkin holder and salt and pepper shakers.
I try to make eye contact.
You avert your eyes.
Those piercing, ice blue,
those beautiful eyes.
I see them every day.
I haven't seen your smile in years.
I look beyond you.
There is an older couple in the booth behind.
I glance to the left and see a row of backs.
Backsides on barstools.
Patrons in for lunch.
Some of them with legs long enough for their feet
to rest flat on the floor.

Wearing loafers, scuffed and weary. Like us.
Some of them with legs too short
for their feet to find the floor.
One even kicked off her shoes and
was swinging her legs back and forth.
Left front. Right back.
Right front. Left back. Repeat.
Repeat.
Repeat.....
Swinging happily.
Existing merrily.
Unlike us.
Waiting for her fried fish platter and coleslaw.
I wondered if she was going to get hushpuppies,
and if they were made there in house
or pulled out of the freezer
and poured from a bag into the fryer.
I turn my attention again to you.
"Are you going to talk to me?" I say.
No response.
"Honey please." I reach for your hand which is on the table.
You pull it away and place it in your lap.
You finally make eye contact.
The contempt hits me like a glass ashtray between the eyes.
Louder, I say your name and ask why.
The waitress appears at my left side with my order.
She asks me who I'm talking to.
That's when I realize she only has one plate.
The older couple in the booth behind sit rigidly.
Her; attempting to hear everything.
Him; watching intently.
All the backs on the barstools are now facing

the other direction.
We have the front sides
of casual business attire and power suits facing our way.
I notice that the girl who was swinging her feet is still at it.
And she is you.
And she smiles.
She gets up from the bar and takes leave while her
comrades stare daggers at me.
I notice that there is a glass of iced tea
sitting at the spot on the bar that you just abandoned,
beads of perspiration silently, slowly making
their way to the bar.
I look across our booth.
No you.
No Iced tea.
Nothing.
I look up at the waitress and ask her to repeat herself.
She asks me who I'm talking to.
I tell her the past.
Everyone loses interest and I ask for an iced tea.

In my madness
I conjure you.
You never fail to come.
In my lucidity, my soul beckons you.
You are a mustard seed, hiding in a crock full of peppercorns.
You were my comfort.
My peace.
My sanctuary.
Now, you are my adversary.
My prison.
My despair.

My anguish.
You are a glance in a funhouse mirror
when jocularity is absent.
You are ten years of failure.
You are the thief with the silver tongue,
the mother of misdirection.
The distractor of the reasonable.
You are a serpent
in a hand basket.
The harbinger of deceit and the wielder of the whitewash.
You are the leaver.
The one who leaves destruction in your wake. And God
help me,
I just want to sit across the table from you and
watch you eat pancakes.

When the Cavalier Shoot Blind

He walked into the bar with a hole in his
soul and a chip on his shoulder.
His tolerant nature had fled him as he was possessed
by the spirit of someone much older.
The olive branch extended could not have
landed on a man much colder.
Give an asshole an inch, they wont even
flinch. It just makes them bolder.
I want to walk through that door and out
of this hell, but I can't say the reason.
I'm sporting your labels and your sheep are so blind,
they don't see what I'm seeing. They're sure to think
me unkind when they find out I'm leaving.
Scapegoats, doormats, patsies and targets
who stand in the crosshairs, surely,
they're guilty of treason.
You were only ever half a person when
we met. I filled in the blanks with
roses and saints, not really knowing you yet.
You come down like a building crushing all. All you
view as a threat. You'd know the difference, We'd
have sidestepped the landmine, had we bothered
vetting the thing we were about to get.

Looking Up at a Blade of Grass

I have seen your intellect and there is
no lack of depth.
Just a heart so stingy that it cannot
spare a breath.
Your beauty is a poison that leaves
me quite bereft.
A poison I have consumed munificently,
and now I buckle under its heft.

I'm looking for the layers,
that you pretend you have.
I'm looking for words
and interesting situations
to put them in.

My tongue is a liar.
My mind is on fire.
I won't surrender,
a slave
to your ire.

I'm looking for worlds on a blade
of grass.

I'll settle for truth
and a glass of milk.
A snifter of vermouth
paints reality in silk.

In silky smooth strokes of
delicious deception.

Oh, how easily a head is turned.
I'm looking for a promise on the back of
the hand that's about to change my
focus.

I'm looking for a reason to trust the snake.

My tongue is a liar.
My mind is on fire.
I'm willing to bite.
Come, let us conspire.

I'm looking for the season that opens my eyes.
I'm looking for the starting line.
I'm looking at my watch.
I'm looking for the other contestants.
I'm looking at vacant spaces and dust.
I'm looking at an audience of one who has
somewhere else to be.

My tongue is a liar.
My mind has retired.
I'm willing to kill dignity for the satisfaction
of desire.

Somewhere out there is a tree under which they've buried me.
The bark is poison to the touch, and the shade
provided isn't much.

It casts a shadow at days end and tames
the wind now and then.
The fruit it yields aint that good. It stands alone in the woods.

I'm looking at your layers
And an interesting situation.
I'm looking at a new world on a blade of grass,
a change of focus,
a different season.
I'm looking at an empty canvas and I'm holding a brush.
And I am remembering that
I don't have to be maimed
in spirit.
I can choose to receive what you have given me
as a gift.
Sometimes the biggest favors that
people do for you come with bruises
and abrasions.

I'm going to press these bruises and pull these scabs.
I will exhume myself
And find a tree that isn't so
You.
I will look for my reflection
in the similarly discarded and
we will whisper; we will let the sorcery that conjures wonder
stick to the roofs of our mouths
like soft white bread.

Free to Fly

To my friend that stands against the wall,
watching what happens from there.
Don't hide in the shadows.
Don't look at the ground.
Don't run from the nobility you bear.

To my friend who has nothing to say,
screaming mightily
in your own mind.
Open your mouth and let it all out
And make peace
with the voice you then find.

To my friend who can't find a way.
Take your hand
and place it on my heart.
It beats for you.
It's strong and it's true.
We're gonna find you a new play and
a new part.

I can see
all the things that are keeping you unfree.
Your anxiety. Your pain. The past and the rain.
C'mon baby, abandon that wall and lean on me.

To my friend who exited today.
I wish
I had said all that before.
You're beautiful.
You're strong.
I've loved you long.
But you've left me behind.
I didn't see the signs.
Now in the rain I'm left with my shame and
baby you're free to fly.

Did You Come to Me in My Darkness

I ride the fences,
looking for a space to fill.
Looking for a purpose to serve.
Watching for the enemy.
Counting the ticks
my pocket watch sounds.
Holding my breath.
Making my rounds.

I trail the lost ones through the brush and the dust.
I smell their fear.
With them, I cry their tears.
I hear the trepidation in their prayers.
I find them.
I lead them home or chase them way.

I look in the mirror and wonder,
Why?
Why do I wander, unchecked?
As lost as my renegades,
but not nearly as missed.
Who comes to lead me, to take my hand?
I would trade my soul for a bridge to cross,
and a heart to follow. But,
I'm not so sure I haven't already dealt it away.

So, I seek comfort between your sheets.
Whispering empty promises
to your heart.
Performing heavy acts on your person.
Hoping pleasure renders you
forgetful.

I want to be had.
I want to be forgotten.
I want my cake and
I want yours.
I will do what I must to take.

Request what you will of me.
Anything physical
that requires an act of touch.
Just don't put me on the inside of those fences that I ride.

I'm the outsider
looking in.
Even when I've been fed and given everything.
(How did that happen, *Boy?*)

Where is your mind?
Hiding in a dark corner?
Hands pressed over its ears.
Eyes shut tight.
Avoiding light.
Or the attention of others.
Meanwhile, the adversary has the reins.

I am the project that never ends.
I am the victim and the oppressor.
I am the lamb.
I am the Unquiet Mind.
And I am the Albatross.

I ride the wind,
in the sky or on the ground.
I ride the fences.

It's cold and lonely,
but contempt is a heavy coat, man.
The sleeves are long, and before long,
you sweat your way into the heat.

So, walk away.
Or have another cup of coffee.
Tepid,
with lots of sugar,
while we laugh about boundaries,
expectations and fences; and the absurdity of forever.

Introducing The Unquiet Mind

The More the Merrier

When I hear the door lock behind me
and I'm standing in the dark.
When the hair on my arms
stands straight up.
And I feel your breath behind in my ear
and I taste it,
fowl, rancid.
When I first feel your fingers
run down the side of my ribcage,
I try not to make a sound.
Then, the calm.
The calm before the storm.
Fear paralyzes me.
I can't turn my head to look back
or move my feet to turn around,
to see if it's really you
and not....
I'm locked in.
I can't move.
I can't see.
I can't speak!

I can hear,
but not a word is being said,
and I can feel you touching me.
If it is you
and not....
I'm locked in, and it is not quiet in my head.

How long must I scream inside
my head.
Scream to wake up.
Scream to break out of this locked box.
How long must I scream in here
to be heard
out there?

"Scream all you want *boy*. You aint ever getting out of here.
We got you now and there's no end to the fun we're going to
have. Not you *boy,* no fun for you. We."

Excuse Me. Could You Not Play Hopscotch on My Cerebral Cortex Today? That Would be Great, Thanks

When I'm at a loss for words.
When hope is absent
and harmony is lost
and love was never anything but a rumor.

When days are long and hot.
When work never ends,
and the tax it places on your body
is a price you cannot continue to pay.

When simple transactions become monumental operations.

When I reach for your hand and you pull it away.
When ice cream tastes like failure.
When kids are slaughtered in a classroom,
or a clinic.
When a different opinion challenges a tenuous grasp on reality.
When the lightest of touches and the most generous of words
assault your tender soul.

When the petal lays you open faster than the thorn.
She will not hold the mirror up in front of you, grab your hair
and force you to look.
She stands in front of it and whispers softly, and then steps aside.
Leaving you
to confront… you.

She is as light as silk when she lays you open.
As light as silk and as stealth as the whip.

Knees were made to bend. She demands nothing less.
She demands it with a whisper and the smile you find on the
face of a friend.
On my knees once again.
Looking up
at a hazy sky and
silently accusing the one I believe (and don't believe)
to be there.

I shake my fist at the sky,
denying the existence
yet praying for rain so the tears go unnoticed.

I can't do this today.

There is nothing left in me. Drag me to the dirt and leave me
there.
Perhaps I will sprout anew tomorrow.

But for now, I care not to evolve.

"Don't you count on it *boy*," it says from somewhere in the back.

"We can cover you in Kiwi Wax or Brasso and rub you with
a cloth all day long. You're still gonna be that same dingy,
tarnished, broken piece of shit you were yesterday. Nothing
anew about you, is there *boy*?"

I turn. "Who the fuck is we?"

The Wake-Up Call

Sunday morning comes like the hunter.
Quiet and deliberate it moves.
And while the maples are
casting their shadows,
the breeze in the leaves stirs in you.

The clock is ticking
away the seconds
and the sheet is quite heavy on your skin.
There's nothing pressing, no ambition.
No project nor work to begin.

As you lay there
and stare at the ceiling,
alone with the ghosts
in your mind,
you can't help saying her name, or
recalling how you defamed,
or what drove you to be so unkind.

Shakey legs carry you to the kitchen.
Yesterday's coffee left in the pot.
Your ashtray is running right over
with half smoked cigarettes,
lit and forgot.

A bottle of bourbon sits on the end table.
Capless,
accusing and rank.

Your rocks glass didn't find a coaster.
Is there anything left in your tank?

She's not coming back
and you know it.
You sit
and light one more butt.
She's been living
three counties over,
content
while you merely live
in this rut.

Out of the corner of your eye you see it.
A cushion over and to the right.
You finger the grip upon it
And wonder why you didn't do it last night.

It's in your hand.
You stare at it blankly.
The trigger was made for your skin.
Eyeing the slide,
the hammer and barrel
it offers its solution again.

"Go ahead *boy*, you know you want to. But all of us over here
on this side, we know you ain't got the hair on your ass
to do it. You want a little help with that?
All you got to do is ask, **Boy**. Just ask.
How interesting am I now?"

Are You Trapped With It? Or...?

The sun is shining through the windshield
As the day meanders west.
And the clouds
are kids in bumper cars.
Bumping with all their best.

And daylight,
that commodity
will soon be spent and gone.
But still,
it illuminates the corn in the field
before it has sung its song.

The day has yielded many miles.
We all endeavor
to make our hay.
Some did it with happy hearts.
The rest did it anyway.

And now,
the quiet time.
The time I need the most.
The shift from industry
to artistry
No pride.
No prejudice.
No boast.

But inspiration's waning and I'm walking on my own.
My mind is a painfully blank canvas,
lost and far from home.
Maybe there's something to be had
from the dark that settles in.
But to wander that ethereal dusk
may conjure the beast within.

He's been quiet for a few weeks,
that unquiet fucking fiend.
And I feel it rage
against its cage
Its want.
Its wrath.
Its need.
And a thought is all it needs.

"Hey *Boy*, it's been a spell. Here comes the pain."

The Walls Make Quite the Echo When Nothing is Being Said

Words fly out of the mist of an inactive mind,
from no point of origin.
No neighboring mind to form them and
no mouth to launch them.

Words uninterrupted.
Words abiding.
Words, ancient.
Long lived,
From ancient battlefields
of sage and clover
where innocence is sacrificed
on the altar of
amour propre, and dominion.
They float and
linger
and bounce about,
propelled by a gentle breeze that
also has no origin
inside these four walls.
No door
through which to steal away.
Heavy words.
Light on the breeze.
Wreaking havoc on the mind, yet
so gentle on the walls. Words like:

You
Sold
Us
Down
The
River.
One of these days.
One of these days.
One of these days.

I will break my chains.
I will break down these Goddamn walls.
And I will refute those heavy fucking words.
The accusation will die and
I will sleep the quiet sleep of the released.
But for now,
Admire with me the chains I just can't shake.

"That's right *boy*, You just keep telling yourself that." it says with sinister satisfaction.

"Yeah, well. I noticed you didn't show up when it was happening. What's the matter? Did she scare the shit out of you too?"

And just like that, the noise in your head will bring you to your knees.

Color Diluted

A palette of vibrant color
and a book of throw away words.
Sleight of hand and misdirection.
A trap door and a mirror.

It emerges from the shadows from time to time
to exchange a few words,
to remind itself that it still can.
To remind itself that it could matter.

When the master extends the brush,
what color are you?
Could you ever call the canvas home?
How large was your little minute?

When the words are read or spoken,
or even just thought,
do you find more steel in your spine?
Or do shadows and trapdoors beckon and
point the way home?

You loathe this
self-imposed,
this exodus.
It is your stigmata.
It is your purge.

Did anyone part the sea before you.
Are the chariots behind you real.
Can you swim?

Your misery.
Your pain.

Your isolation.
Your stripes.

Your absolution.

I guess the life of a recluse
has its perks.
You lucky devil, you.

Hey *boy*, look at me when I'm talking to you.

Life Lived in Hindsight.

I passed a storefront window and stopped when I caught
my reflection in the glass.
You were standing beside me, pointing.
I took two steps back and one two the side.
The sun was in a different place.
The angle had changed.
I was now looking through the glass at a mannequin dressed
for the beach and wearing a hat similar to something
in your closet.
Our reflections were no longer there.
I looked to my left, you were gone as well.

I side stepped again and approached this window, this glass.
This heartless fucking mirror.
Again, I was there. You were not.
Where did you go?
Don't answer that, I'm quite well aware of where you are.
Don't you love it when people say,
"Things happen for a reason."
"When one door closes…"
Yeah.
Do me a favor with your cliché', daily affirmation
talking points bullshit.
Try taking a person's pulse before
you start spewing that crap.

"You can't live your life in hindsight."

I drive these highways and
walk these county roads and
saunter up amazing city streets.
And I see places where we were together,
and places that I should have gotten you to.

But you, little ghost,
you follow me.
Everywhere.
I am tethered to your memory,
like a mother strings her child's mittens
through the sleeves of its coat.
Little ghost.
Not gone.

Life lived on autopilot.
Life lived in hindsight.
Maybe I understand masochism
better than I think I do.
Why don't you crawl out of the shadows
and say something?
I'll turn that other thing off for a bit.

"Hey *boy,* you…"
I said shut up.

Curiosity and Kerosene

Love is not lost that never bloomed.
Show me where it hurts, I'l find a rat to dress your wounds.
Is it really dead were it never tombed?
My callous demeanor was well taught and well groomed.

I will mend the fences I must mend,
reinforce the walls I must defend,
interpret the many cues that you send,
and pay no mind to the heartstrings that you bend.

The gifts you gave me are quite keen.
I have the soul of a machine.
My intentions are obscene, yet my speech is laced with
saccharine.
I no longer feel what you swear to me is real.
For what I cannot bargain I'm so happy just to steal.

You are the ghost I cannot shake.
You are the truth I cannot fake.
You are the lie I tell my people for my own serenity's sake.

I am the bone you quietly broke.
I am the butt of all your jokes.
I loathed your Godcamn chains and I resented your
Goddamn yoke.

Incendiary fever dreams.
I swim in pools of kerosene.
We snuff the flame with Vaseline and taunt the god of evergreens
with porcelain mugs of coffee and cream.

I bray to him
like an ass.
Pray he shows me........

"Hey *Boy!*
What the fuck are you whining about now? Braying like an ass.
That's the only thing you said that's accurate. Don't you realize
that currently, nobody here wants to hear it. In this great big old
world *Boy*, it's just you and the mirror, and me. And let me tell
you something else, that fucking mirror has it out for you. How
is it that you just hold on to that shit with a death grip?" says
the Unquiet Mind.

"Oh yeah? You ought to thank your lucky stars that I hold on
to that shit with a death grip. Did it ever occur to you that I'm
the host with the most? Where do you go If I let it go? You like
to say that I can't live without you, how bout we go choose
you a new vessel? Hmm? Maybe something on a ventilator?
Something lobotomized? Something with four or five of your
brothers and sisters running around in its cranium? Would you
like that? Give up some head space, some of that autonomy to
go be just a number in the crowd? C'mon shit bird, let's go to
the asylum, get you a new zip co........"

The scream in his head was as deafening as if he were standing
next to a firehouse whistle, and quite unexpected it brought
him to his knees. He wasn't going anywhere today, or the rest of
the week. That's how he knew he had won this round.

You know you're fucked in this life when everything you win
hurts every bit as badly as everything you lost.

Killing Time in my Mind

Physically, I walk alone.
Standing on corners.
Staring into storefront windows,
They're just other fun house mirrors
where I kill time in my mind.

I kill time
in my mind
where I'm never alone.
Dimensions.
Dementia.
A million miles away,
right around the corner from home.

And I hide in plain sight
in this waking world
where vulnerability
is the veil on me.
Killing time in my mind
In dark little corners,
I'm a schooner made of paper, drowning in turbulent seas.

Unusual venues
play host to the ubiquitous shadows
that are common guests in my head,
At some point I expect her
(The spectre)
To step out of those shadows
And convince me I'm better off dead.

But for now, in my mind
I shall kill time instead.

I'm killing time in my mind.
I'm killing it slow.
I'm tasting every wretched little piece.
I'm killing the past.
She's not but a rumor.
She's a bitch.
She's a barn.
She's the beast.

And I'm still in my quiet corner,
dining fine
and killing time.
Surrounded by many and completely alone.
Remembering assaults,
and far away classrooms.
Allowing my rage to bleach bones.
Letting my bitter
astringent wrath
fuck with the piece in my home.

That thousand-yard stare
I'm looking right through,
I see the spectre again.
I'm killing time in my mind,
slamming the door on the past,
determined to not let her back in.

"Hey *boy*. What makes you think you can keep me out?"

Creeping in the Periphery

Sabotage in pretty paper and eloquent speech.
Promises breathlessly whispered,
but never meant to keep.
Hollow, empty gestures echo in abandoned rooms.

Flashbacks to childhood nightmares. The kind that won't let
you open your eyes because you're terrified of seeing in the
waking world what's destroying you behind those eyelids.

They couldn't pull that sheet out of your clenched, knotted
fingers. Your grip was so tight.

The weight of the world was on your chest.
Every breath making you thinner.
Every breath, a stolen moment.
Every breath, a fugitive in shadows.

Bovidae on the bank watching the crocodile
work the heard.
You know what happens when you've drawn your last.
When you stop moving.

Open your eyes.
Open your eyes!
Draw a fucking breath!
"Oh. Hey!
What are you doing here?"

"What do you think I'm doing here, *boy*? I'm here to feed. We, are here to feed."

It's so close. You don't know where you end and it begins.

"Hey *boy*, close those eyes again and don't you move. You keep moving like that, I won't be able to get my mouth around your shoulders."

They swallow you whole
while you are hyper-aware
through the entire humid, sticky consumption.

Your metaphors are armed and hungry.
They stomp through the dark.
They laugh, they devour.
They mimic and sell scrutiny but deliver only chains.
And you are helpless, unresistant to overture
providing distraction.
Resistant to self-preservation.

Resistant to the other side of the eyelids.

"I always knew I could count on you, *Boy*. Blind is blind, even when it's voluntary"

Slipping the Mooring on a Schooner Called Neurosis

Are you lost?
Or do you know something the
rest do not?

When you want desperately to engage
and just as desperately to hide,
and find yourself incapable of doing either,
are you lost?
Or do you know something
the rest do not?

When your meals taste of rust,
when the only color you see is beige,
when the gentle breeze blows out your focus,
when everything is the most
and everything is the least.
When everything has changed
and everything is the same,
are you lost?
Or do you know something
The rest do not?

When you talk to ghosts, or worse,
yourself in disguise.
That flagitious,
odious, dirty thing that insists
that you've always been unworthy of
the contempt that it takes to
consider you.

When you look in the mirror
and you see someone else's face
because you are not sure who you
are not,
or who you are.
When that face stares back at you,
beige, unfocused and smelling of rust,
Do you run?
Are you lost?
Do you know something
the rest do not?

Is it you in the mirror?

"Hey *boy*. Why don't you reach out and touch the glass? Put your mind at ease. Go ahead. Extend that arm. What have you got to lose? I dare you?"

Who's gonna blink first?
Is today the day?
What happens when you reach out
and there is nothing to be gained?
No insight.
No possession.
No connection.
No bonds.
Nothing tethering you to a position,
or a soul.
What happens when you're light
on the exterior
but your soul is as black as tar?

"Hey *boy,* that just makes you my kind of people. It means I've done my job well. I aint ever letting you go *boy.* I bet you didn't know this, but there are things blacker than tar. I'm gonna show you *boy.* Are you lost? Do you want to run? Relax, *boy,* at the very least, you know something the rest do not.

The Albatross, Unsalvageable

Can I bag my crazy?
Put it in the sack?
Take it to customer service
And get my money back?

"Hey *boy*.
What's the matter?
Got yourself a little writer's block?
A little obstacle to the
old thought process?
You got nothing to say, do ya *boy*?
What makes today any different
than any other day?
It's not like anyone listens to you anyway.

Until now.
You don't know how to deal with it,
do ya *boy*?
You bought all that garbage
They like to spew about you.
You know why you bought it?
Cause deep down, you knew they were right.

C'mon *boy*, say it with me,
Anyone that has anything nice to say
about you
is lying to you.
Just ask Mom and Dad.

Compliments can't be trusted,
and the ones who paint them,
paint them in blood.
Daddy's gone,
and Mama doesn't remember now
what a disappointment you were to her.

But you stick with me *boy*. I got the past straight and
I will always tell you the truth.

You're as worthless today
as you were back then.
What's that?
Is that a sigh of relief I hear?
Release?
I told *boy*, I'm here for you"

Are the bats in your belfry Carefree?
Do they make a joyful sound?
Do you crave their company
when no one else is around?

Is there some kind of relief you find
in keeping yourself alone?
Is solitude where you hang your hat?
Is desolate the ground you call home?

You believe in God.
He speaks to you in dreams.
He's tender towards your every care and
quick to mend your seams.

"Is that right *boy*?
You believe in God?
God looks out for you?
You have the faith of a grain
of a mustard seed?
Tell you what, *boy*.
I will concede that there may be a God
if you will concede that there
may not.
Reluctant, are we?
Well, it is a leap *boy*.
You remember when they told you about
Santa Clause,
Or the Easter Bunny?
You remember when they told you they
were just kidding, but by no means
Were you to tell your little brother?
And then they laid Jesus on you.
Hoooo.
But Jesus is absolutely real, right?
You fuck up, Santa don't bring you no presents.
This works till you're nine or ten.
Once they take that away from you,
once you've been conditioned,
they hit you,
they control you,
they break you with Hell."

"Hey shit brick", I say under my breath.
"When was the last time you walked in and out of Heaven?
The only reason you are willing to concede
that there might be a God is because

you are ancient.
You know he's there
because you have stood before him.

"Well *boy*, that is an interesting theory.
Ha ha ha.
The accusations you level at a figment
of your imagination. Sooo entertaining.
He may be there.
He may not.
I'll never tell.

And neither will he.
Because when the pilot light goes out *boy*,
you'll either stand before him
looking at one of two destinations,
or the worms will eat,
and you will draw nothing but a long,
prolonged, eternal black blank."

One day you woke
and your world had changed.
You had more stroke
so you rearranged.
You dropped that hooded cloak
unwilling to hide.
Say goodbye to the Turkey Oak,
Say hello to the beast inside.

You cleaned house and you threw away
the one who cared,
the one who stayed.
He held you up
day after day.

You put him down
like a mangy stray.
You put him down
every day.
You put him down,
down he'll stay.

"Like I said *boy*. The whole world will abandon you,
but I will always be here, and I will listen.
Because I got a thing for the broken,
the twisted,
the unsalvageable.
That's you *boy*! Unn-salvageable."

Smoke and Deception

"Hey *boy*. You're looking a little sluggish today. You look like the Sandman never showed. That's too bad *boy*. It aint easy sleeping with all that racket going on in your head."

"I told you, you aint getting out of here. We gonna have too much fun with you, *son*."

"Oh. I'm sorry. Am I a little loud? And what was that question you asked; 'Who the fuck is we?'? Who the fuck do you think you are? We are you, *boy*. But not that little bitch version you like to play. You, and your Tumbleweed, and your fucking Albatross. Is that right *boy*? Everything in your head traveling?"

"What about me? Just like you, I aint going nowhere either."

"Do you know who I am *boy*? Do you know how I got here?"

I can't be bothered to look at it. I know it better than it knows itself. I just keep my face pointed down at the notepad in my lap, scribbling away, looking as timid as the day is long. And I'm also watching. Intently. From my corner across the room. Where a fly on the wall is worth all the birds in all the bushes.

It's clearing its throat to speak. I turn my head in its direction. It comes up short. I get up and step towards it.

"I know who you are. How could I not? I created you."
"You? You created me? That's…"
"That's right. I created you."
"Who do you think you are?!" it bellows.

I take another step forward and lightly chuckle.

"You know exactly who I am, because I created you. And the only reason you're still around is because I haven't dismissed you yet. I still find you interesting enough to keep around. Like a dog on a leash. I did create you. And you are at least smart enough to know what that makes me. You can snarl all the threats you want, denigrate my character in all the filthy ways that occur to you. I have even allowed you to put your hands on my person. But, in the end you howling little chimp, we both know that *You* are terrified of *me*, because you know who I am, what I am, in this place, in my head. *You* are the Unquiet Mind. I made you."

I'm now standing in front of it, peering intently over it. Towering over it.

"I can unmake you, and it will not be pleasant. So, if you know what's good for you **Boy**, You best announce to the world, in this place, who I am."
"Who am I?"

It whispers unintelligibly.

"I didn't hear you chimp, who am I?"

"You're God." it whispers.

"Who?"

"You are God." It says more clearly.

"Whose God?"

It hesitates.

"Whose God am I!!" I thunder at it.

"Mine, mine, mine. You're my God in this place, in all places. Please don't unmake me….."

"I am your God, just as the one that created me is mine. Don't you forget it. The only power you ever had or ever will have, I gave you. Don't you forget that. The moment you overstep your boundary, the second you cease to be interesting, I will unmake you. And because I'm petulant, the process will be unpleasant. And amusing to me. Do you understand?"

It shakes its head.

"Then go for now."

Back in my little corner, confrontation over for now. Once again scribbling about seabirds and wind driven shrubbery, I think the word "Ni" as I feel the Unquiet Mind seething. And plotting. It knows that I know that it is quite certain that I will never act on the threat. It's also shocked that today wasn't the day. It's just waiting for the day that I allow it to destroy me. I am too.

The Albatross, Unsalvageable II

"You know what, Shit Bird?
I remember you.
How could I not?
You're the same thing
that would come and
whisper in my ear
as I would drink every ounce of
alcohol I could possibly
consume on a nightly basis.
You know what the difference
between now and then is?
All those years ago, you owned me.
Now I own you.
Fuck off! I owe you nothing."

And now for something sure to make you scratch your head and say, Huh?

Fun with Haiku!

Fun with Haiku

In For a Pound

Find a hand to hold.
I am your conspirator.
In for a penny!

Fun with Haiku

In Pieces

Every piece of you,
Stirs well, every piece of me.
Stirring, I am stirred.

Fun with Haiku

What Happens in Your Field

Rapeseed blooms brilliant,
While wild indigo edges.
They tease, please. They blush.

Stacked Haiku

The Tongue: Harbinger of Pleasure and Pain

The back of her hand
Lacked the efficiency found
concealed in her tongue.

No mere appendage.
It does her brain's wet work well.
Venom unleashed kills.

Kills not with kindness.
Destroys no flesh, eats no cell.
The walking corpse weeps.

Empty Nest

Oh Alabama,
The empty rest feels strange.
But it liberates.

Oh Alabama,
naked is a by-product
of your new freedom.

Dear Alabama,
music is a companion.
Hold her hand and dance.

Silence also serves.
Love her, she is your sister.
Plot with her in joy.

Oh Alabama.
Read and paint, make the world yours.
Creator. Master.

Oh Alabama.
Exercise the fiend, junk food.
Sleep your sleep soundly.

Dear Alabama.
Both kids away at college.
Look at what you did!

Sweet Alabama,
She's a builder of nations.
Skip the cereal, Mom.

Fun with Haiku

Repellant Religion

Oh Alabama.
She's unwilling to be crossed.
Her resolve moves me.

Fun with Haiku

Have Another Mushroom

When one wields a shield,
should it protect what's before
as well as what's aft?

Stacked Haiku

The Apple Bites Back

Preserve me in wax.
Peel away the blemishes.
Reveal me as new.

Reveal me as you.
The better half of the whole.
I bathe in your scent.

Ethos, desire.
Head back. "Dive deep!", she whispers.
The apple bites back.

Extinguish the flame.
We'll both be driven senseless.
Pleasure seeks escape.

Pleasure seeps from pores.
Stoma eager to accept.
Tongue tastes, mouth collects.

The violation
you crave with moistening lips
will change everything.

I will be your slave,
willingly exposed for you.
The Apple bites back.

Stacked Haiku

Circles

Circles moving round.
The silence defeating sound.
Churning fertile ground.

Had me at first sight.
I knew it was flight or fight.
Bones and blood, so tight.

What could have been, was.
What did not happen, did not.
Circles moving round.

It is as it is.
It is as it always was,
and as it should be.

Stacked Haiku

Alabama Gives

Oh, Alabama!
The stripes you endure, flesh sings,
songs of submission.

Oh, Alabama.
A porcelain sacrifice,
The gods are well pleased.

Stacked Haiku

A Different Game of Chess

My deceptions come
tangy and fragrantly sweet,
whispered in your ear.

You lick wanting lips
tasting my marmalade lies.
Eyes wide shut, willing.

Compliant, open.
Pleased to taste the citrus ruse.
It sticks to your chin.

You look up knowing,
Lips close on viscous nectar.
Tongue savors its lie.

You were never fooled.
The pitcher plant snares the fly.
Always, I was yours.

Fun with Haiku

The Female Spine

The dividing line.
The Flesh it fields, perfection.
That grand stage denied.

Sugar Preserves

The jar overflows.
Pleasure has a shelf life.
Jam lasts forever.

Attitude Adjustments

Permission to touch.
Permission for everything.
Let's fuck like animals.

The Verbose Boy Drives By

Oh Alabama,
Tuscaloosa lives in haste.
I shall pass, the same.

Ice crystal Clarity

When I haiku,
I speak in ribbons of thrift.
Austerity's voice.

Love, Hate Relationship with Sex and Pain

What I have to say
is noise, and not short nor sweet.
How will you mute me?

If Verbose is a Dirty Word, Spank Me

Oh, Alabama,
your mute button captures me.
It drives the sour out.

How will you mute me?

Fingers in my mouth.
Hands sliding under my waistband.
Eyes locking on mine.

Alternative Alarm Clock

Tongue traces your lips.
Your fingers laced in my hair.
Pushing the button.

Theft

For Whom the Bell Tolls.
The Pit and the Pendulum.
To a God Unknown.

Parched Lips and Willing Hips

When water trumps wine.
When fucking all night breeds peace.
I'm at your cervix.

Supplication

I am on my knees.
Service to you, my passion.
For now, I am yours.

And Now For More
Of The Completely
Expected

Chicken Pie

She burns passion. She is light.
The forces within her can make or break you.
She will lament neither. You earned your disposition.

She is a crystal coated tree, branches swaying,
dancing in the winter storm.

She is the gale driving ocean to rock.
She is every color of autumn against the bluest sky.

She is 28,000 sunsets kissing the sky passionately,
Coaxing it to blush in fiery red and pink hues of desire.

She is every shade of Iris.
Go, be the dirt that nurtures her.
Grab her by the waist.
Push her against the wall and kiss her.
Kiss her.
Like a ravenous, empty-handed hunter,
stumbling across a campfire and a simmering pot
of aromatic promise.
(Chicken Pie anyone?)

She is beautiful. Tell her so. Often.
Say it with your eyes, Say it with your hands,
your mouth,
your flesh.

When she gives you the to do list, grab her by the heart as well.
Then, give her yours.

Propper Submission

I've always been willing to see
What you've been willing to
show me.
And,
I've always been willing to
risk your annoyance,
by daring to look
behind the curtain at the things
you didn't want me to see.
because how else
can I know you?

I've always been willing to stand where
You have been willing to plant me.
But,
I've also been willing to stand beside you,
in front of,
or behind you.

I've always been willing to be quiet
when you would rather I not
raise my voice.
But,
I will shout down with the volume of legions those
that would intrude upon your peace.

You are the piece and
then you are the puzzle.
You are the fragment and
then you are the whole.
Without the smallest piece of you,
you will always only be *almost*.
Without the smallest piece of you, I will always only be *almost*.

I will always look for your reflection in my life.
On the calmest of lakes,
or in the smallest, sharpest shards
of a broken mirror.
Lead, follow or stand beside me,
I don't care.
Soft or sharp edges,
I don't care.
As long as I can reach out and write my name in the grit,
on your pieces.

You Are Saffron

We are now an
eclectic collection
of emotional carpet baggers.
Tumbleweeds.
Beautiful losers.

People who have settled
in the past
and have found themselves incapable of trust
on a sustained basis.
Lines become blurred.
Timidity never walks in greener grass.

It wasn't always that way. But still,
We want.
We crave.
We need.
We need that hand on our ribcage in the morning,
that hand pulling you closer
for a few, wonderful little minutes…
of fiction.

Oh, how we settle for fiction.

We have been philanthropists
With our attention, giving it to those
that we thought worthy.

Some of us hoping to receive a measure in return,
forgetting that philanthropy is its own reward,
and becoming empty for the experience.
Looking with envy on those
who have a heart of beating stone.

Will you ever find your forever person?
Or are you restricted to life in the library,
knowing only as temporary
your possession
of the novels
you are able to put your hands on.
Knowing only as temporary
lives that you've touched.
Hoping to break free of the lend/lease
side of intimacy,
to set aside your carpet bag
and breathe the air of the
claimed.

You tumbleweeds,
stand still.
You are not second best,
you are not yesterday's news.
You are not bargain-basement merchandise.

You are saffron.
Bright.
Bold.
Sweet.
You are a
yellow rose.
You are forever,
and someone out there
is forever
for you.

She is a Counterweight Unaware

I didn't know I was going to
need you like I do.
You are a sexton and the stars.
You're not just another in a
long line of passers through.
From you,
there is no need to hide these scars.

I've traveled deliberately in circles
around my cage,
and I pause between the seasons
to seethe.
But you've come around and swept away
my senseless rage,
and given me a reason to believe.

You are the joy
of soil under nails.
And you are the harvest in the fall.
I am the sailor
who has found his white whale,
and I am the envy of those who have it all.

Many hours have I wasted
licking wounds no longer there,
and feeling the lash of abuses,
ancient
and noticed only by me.
You've come along and showed me
new places to put my cares.
You've brought tranquility to my turbulent
and furious seas.

So, walk
on the waters that churn
and turn
my anxiety. Walk atop my seas, my love.
Walk right in and claim it with your style and grace.
Come wear my reverence like a glove.

Because,
you are the joy
of soil under nails.
And you are the harvest in the fall.
I am the sailor who has found his white whale.
and, I am the envy of those who have it all.

She is the Stand

When love and understanding
are the shields you choose to defend me.
When I'm cold
I would sooner have your arms wrapped
around my neck
than that bright and trendy scarf.
And put your lips near my ear.
So close I can feel the humidity in your breath
when you whisper the affirmations
you know I need...

And know,
that smile melts every ice crystal that
formed the box around my heart.
No storm can stand against you, my champion.
You are my heart and my blood.
I was never worthy of your solicitude,
But I was always grateful to wear it.

Centerpiece

When words rarely escape you
and then they do.
When you never fail to think rationally
about what is to come and
then you do.
When you know you have been caught
and you never want to be set free.

Not another day.
Not another hour.
Not another meal without you.
You are the centerpiece.
I can hear you smile.
You are the centerpiece of my life,
and I am going to build my world
around you.

I can hear you smile.
And I know you can feel
what I will never say.
I know you know me.
On this table you are the centerpiece.
There's no color,
no flavor.
no verve without you.

Without you
there is only motion.
Without you
grace never breathed,
she never laughed,
she never cried.
She caught the bus to the city and
she came home.
never once having opened her eyes.
Never once using her nose.
Never once hearing the symphony.

Without you
my gray matter remains singularly
focused only on the distance
I am required to cover.
It doesn't chase distractions.
It reaches for no joy.
It tastes no sweet or savory.
It lives,
but it lacks life.

Bring me loud vibrant color.
Bring me joy.
Bring me humor.
Bring me triumph, or defeat.
Bring me loss.
Bring me pain.
Bring me love.
The thorns and the petals.
I am the canvas.
I am the cloth.
And I am blank.
I am empty without you.
I am the table.
Set.

White linen cloth and napkins,
austerely set with heavy silver
and uninspiring flatware.
You are the centerpiece.
Bring the fire, bring the flavor, bring the joy.

Conspirator Fugitive and the Beaten Path

Follow me through the back door,
down the stairs
and past the gardens.
Follow me past the chicken coop and
over the property line.
Follow me through the pasture,
over the gently rolling hills.
to the tree line,
to the big white pine that once grabbed me by the seat of my
pants
and wouldn't let go.
Follow me to the magical forest
where anger and animosity
dare not tread. They hang by the tree line,
waiting for my return.
Listen to the brook babble
as it makes its way to the Cathance,
that taker of small children. Ricky Munsey. We remember.
Hear the birds alert the other inhabitants
to our presence, just like they always did
in this place where I hide.

See the lady slippers and
the mushrooms.
Smell the fragrant beckoning
of the pine and the flowers.

Taste the blackberries.
Let the juice stain your lips.
Feel the thorns.
Let the scent of joy and anxiety
intermingle on this organic stage
that has been set for you.
Say hello to my old friends
as they approach from the mist,
wagging their tails and panting.
Excited for me to crouch down and
rub their ears as they
lick away the tears.
oh man.

Strip the years away.

To all of you things that move,
what moves you?

To the migratory spirit,
beast or bird,
feeding on sap or sweet nectar.
Feeding on the fallen or caught.
To the vagabond counting his change.
The tramp who runs,
who raids laundry lines
and lunch boxes.
To the burnt in spirit.
To the broken runner.
To those under the compulsion of ancient, inner voices.
To those propelled by exterior forces…

Where is your sanctuary?
What aroma brings you peace?
What door will we open?
What threshold shall we cross?
I am in you,
and you are in me.

Never look back
past that tree line,
up the hill and over the pasture.
Lean on the big white pine.
Allow your hands to be stuck in its sap.
Struggle not against it.
And, if you stay here with me,
I will stay here with you,
caught in my own trap.
Happy to be crushing on old memories.
Bound with you.
Bind me to you.

Hiding in Plain Sight.

I was in the corner
Hiding in plain sight.
Veiled by the shadows.
Looked passed.
Looked through.
And absolutely fine with it.

It was dark and the place was kind of swanky,
playing some cool jazz on the sound system.
Tony Bennett, Sinatra, if that's jazz.
I don't mind that sort of change of pace.
I wouldn't have been surprised if Van Morrison
had snuck in a Moondance.
It was lively there, and the patrons were younger than me,
by decades.
I've waited a long time to write that line. It feels comfortable.
I listened to them from my corner.
No more noticeable to them than an unremarkable
painting on the wall.
I didn't interact. I was writing. I was watching my
biography spill out before me.
And waiting for my meal.

I watched them live their lives as I hid in plain sight.

I wasn't bitter or in a bad place. I wasn't writing my obituary.
It just occurred to me that,
I was completely alone, but surrounded by all of this
wonderful noise,
this chaos.
Surrounded by all these wonderful people,
this amalgamation of humanity,
Who had suspended their daily apprehensions
to come out and smile at one another.

I was hiding in plain sight.
No more noticeable than a painting on the wall.
A chameleon against the tree, only moving
to lick his eye occasionally.
It was the first breath of relief that I had been able to breathe.
A breath that didn't belong to you.

I hide in plain sight.
I'm a fixture covered in dust.
I lay in wait.
Nothing distracts the patient serpent.
It sits so still
in plain sight.

Little Pieces of Me

I have placed little pieces of me in this box for you.

Not necessarily the ones I want
to give you.
Certainly not the pieces that define me.

But, they are pieces of me
that you can wrap your hands around.

Things that I have touched.
Things that have touched me.
Things that you are now touching,
things that are now touching you.

Not the things I wanted to give you first.
A conversation across the table,
a walk through an outdoor market or
a look behind the curtain.
A proper introduction to the things that
move me.
From where
they move me,
from within.

You will not find what is behind my eyes
in this box.
There is no love or lunacy within,
No pool to drown in.
It's a box with dimensions, but it has no depth.

What it does have
are little p eces of me.
Breadcrumbs.
Innuendo.
Whispers that never see the light of day.

It doesn't have what you'll find
behind my eyes.
Just whispers,
and dirt, and little pieces of me.

All the Little Minutes

Your strength is acquired while your face is buried in your hands,
lamenting all the little minutes that bent you
but did not break you.
If you can,
cherish them as well.
You are a miracle.
A beast and a saint, as you should be.
You are the master of all your little minutes.

Embers Under Toes.

The present is a leaky faucet.
It drips with wrath.
We long for other seasons
with no casualties
and the absence of wrath.
I hadn't noticed your ghost
had come to visit.
When it has worn out its welcome,
when your obligation to it has been assuaged, call on me.
Naked, shameless, and satiated,
we will pander to our better spirits
in the moonlight,
dancing
by the dancing fire.

The Feather Wields the Hammer

Her voice, mellifluous.
It breaks away with the grace of a feather on the breeze.
So gentle, the bird knows not its departure.
But her speech.
Salient.
She will enlighten you. She means that shit.
And the sweet dervish like feather that pirouettes
weightlessly to earth
lands with the force of an anvil.
Now, I want her. I want the feather.
I consign myself to the anvil, I consent to her forgery.
She brings the hammer down. The feather wields the hammer.
The blemishes fade.
I am made new.

Looking Through Me

You can wrestle with a truth your entire life.
You can know emphatically,
beyond any doubt at all
that the thing is true
and convince yourself in many of
the little minutes
that the thing is not.
The middle of the road is no place to walk, and I am not
inferior to anyone.

The Beast Wants No Pearls

Offer beast
its heart's delight,
skin fair beneath the moon.
Lift your chin
so throat does pulse,
bite inducing swoon.

Huh?

Euphemisms as currency? Get out!
He never met a metaphor
he didn't like.
He likes them better than people.
To his credit,
he likes dogs
better than either.

The Unobtainable

You stand beyond my reach.
But I will never stop reaching.

Your intellect dwarfs my own.
I will learn.
Your justice is a patient, rolling boil.
It's application, I will earn.
You are a treasure worthy of security.
I must take you and hide you behind my walls.
I am a mimic, prepared to become you, to bathe in your humanity.
Maybe, I can't reach you.
Maybe you won't let me.
But I will continue to display my admiration
in pillars of marble praise.

In Defense of Savagery

The first step is always the hardest.
Your resolve must be harder.
Toe the line.

The antagonist before you are sheep.
The antagonist in the mirror, the wolf.
Toe the line.
You are the very thing the sheep fear.
Nash your teeth and howl!!
Show the world that beautiful, hungry savage!
Leave that line in the dust and take as many throats
as are foolish enough to cross you.

We Bring it on Ourselves

One day, I showed God
exactly who I was.
He took note.
From that day to this
He has been showing me
His sense of justice
and humor.

I am Not in Line

Tortured.
Treasonous.
Villainous.
Reasonless.
Almost a pitiful thing.

Ravenous.
Frivolous.
Completely unchivalrous.
I've no interest in kissing your ring.

Hello Ruby in the Dust

We evolve.
We are not the same people
we were last month,
last week,
yesterday or ten minutes ago.

If your character is strong
and your motives are pure
and you are willing to lead,
I will follow.

Try Me

I would break any promise I ever made to anyone.
I would walk naked through fields of thorn, covered in honey,
tempting those that sting.
There isn't a line I wouldn't cross, a bridge I wouldn't burn,
a fortune I wouldn't steal to get next to you.
I would be your fool.
your knight,
your criminal,
your saint,
your blunt instrument,
to bend your ear and look you in the eyes;
for five minutes of your time.
Because you are the stars before me.
You are the lake reflecting moonlight.
You stir me You feed me.
I need to touch your sou as you have touched mine.

Tearaway Bravado

He's the kind of person
that would dance on a limb
to see if it would bear
his body weight.

Truth be told,
the whole damn tree would fall
were it tethered to his ego.

Empty Grace Notes

Leaders speak in riddles.
Won't look you in the eye.
Their speech consists of grace notes.
They leave you high and dry.

Motivate Me

Some find happiness and productivity quite compatible.
Others can't accomplish a Goddamn thing
till misery eases up behind them,
grabs a handful of their hair, licks the back of their ear and growls,
"Now and forever, you're mine, **bitch!!**
I serve a shadowed master.
I surrender.
Pain equals joy and it is delicious.

Are We Going to Pray

Home is an allusion, a broken promise in your eyes.
That's why I look right through you and beyond
your thin disguise.

You are a master of the games
you play.
You play none you may not win.
I rolled the dice to keep you here,
to watch you come again.
You took it as a sign of weakness.
I knew nothing of your treachery.
Malignancy veiled beneath
Perfidiously meek and lovely eyes.
A bat to the back of the knees.
Yes, you brought me to my knees.

Under Your Spell

I wonder, has anyone ever been able to say "no" to you?
To look up into those eyes, to see you looking down,
to see the mouth that beckons,
the mouth that smiles,
to interpret your spirit as it beguiles,
To feel your breath on their face,
the tips of our fingers, fine as lace
as they move from stomach to throat in their seductive,
sultry pace?
Has anyone ever been miserable enough to tell you no?
I would lose everything, start over with nothing.
I would suffer your bite.
Expose my vulnerability, sacrifice my blood. And my breath.
I would show you my back, a pristine canvas.
I would avert my eyes.
I would say to you the one word that could stop time.
Yes.

It Aint all Saltwater Taffy and Daffodils

The world doesn't want you
the same way that you want it.
You want it functional.
It wants you broken.

You spend time to fix it.
It sends things to break you.

The world spins in exactly the way
It was designed to spin.
The world is not broken,
we are.

Because I Can't

I couldn't walk away from you
baby if I tried.
I'd live longer without water than without you.
Every little thing you bring to the table is life.
I don't want to see you cry, I don't to break your heart,
and I don't want to live without you.
And yes, we can be beasts, but not without charm.
One devil who heals, one angel who harms.
We can sit here just killing time. You take your shot,
baby I'll take mine.
Maybe we'll miss the mark, miss it by a mile.
We may be victims, we may be beneficiaries
of conflicting styles.
I have seen my life without you in it,
and baby that's enough for me.
I couldn't walk away from you
if I tried
and the day you quit me darling,
will be the day the sunshine died.

The Dirty Truth

It's not you being right
that bothers me,
that turns me into an asshole.

It's me being wrong.

You, With the Eyes That Dance!
(RK)

There is something in that woman.
To touch it, I'm dying.
Her smile is like sunshine,
her eyes
of cyan.

Compromising the integrity of my will,
breaking it down to powder.
Through my fingers it spills, I can't live without her.

That woman has something, ancient and wise.
She creates with her heart; she laughs with her eyes.
She restores my faith, everyday by the hour.
She is light, she is water, I can't live without her.

Make me love you in all the ways I haven't.
Make me love you in all the ways I don't.
Make me love you in all the ways I can love no one else.

You may say, "I shouldn't have to make you."
Rest assured, you don't.
It's a compulsion.
No one makes you breathe.

Climbing Down

It is the insinuation of what you are that I surrender to.
The hint.
The whisper.
The rumor.

Within are worlds,
inexhaustible with promise.

Whether I'm a caller,
companion,
or prisoner,
I am content in the warmth of your understanding and
passion.

I am obsequious to my chains.
I am going nowhere.

Aural Tease

I could have sworn
I heard her smile.
Her voice is warm,
it does beguile.

Pieces, Not Broken

Even in pieces,
she is complete.
Shards of her are equal
to the whole that is
anyone else.

Bagworm Diplomacy

Saying that you mean something to me
would be like saying,
"Oxygen, I suppose I need it."
I never agreed to become what I was in
your circle.
I also never refused to become it.
I end myself ever night hoping to wake up the next morning
a little less me. And a lot less you.
It is said that cats have nine lives.
Is anyone of those lives an improvement over the one that
proceeded it?

I suspect that we are all just individuals trapped
in a colony of bagworms.
Our touch is toxic to the outside world.
And, with every rebirth, we find ourselves hopelessly
back in the bag.

Between the Curtains and the Glass

I want to taste your sweat
and desperation.
I want to see it hanging
heavy in the air.
I want to feel its weight
bearing down on me.
I want to pull it right off
of your skin.
Let's use each other, little one.
Let's hide behind the drapes and eat the forbidden fruit.
Let's wallow in the sticky sugar.
I want to lck the juice
off your chin.

At Your Pleasure

I have written a thousand lines tonight.
I wrote them all for you.
I have erased every one of them.
Again,
this I did for you.
Sometimes, all I can do is tell you,
and sometimes
only a demonstration will do.
So, expose that warm, inviting flesh
and tell me when to breathe.
Take what is yours and tell me what is mine.
I can taste you in the air.

Caucasian Rain Dance

My father knew how to make it rain.
Farmers with dry fields would come
from miles around and beg him
to say the words
that would open the skies for days.
And these were the words;
"Hey boys. Throw the tent in the truck, we're going camping."

Philosophy 101

That which does not kill us only makes us pissier.

Shadows and Currents

You may be gone, but your shadow is still on my wall.
Whispering to me,
as silently as driftwood passes by
in the current.

As stealthily as you left.

Men have two muses.
The one that broke them, and the one they believe can
restore their broken pieces.

I will find other beautiful shadows
to paint over you with.
And I will be broken by them too.
And as they break me,
you will finally and silently
slip away in the current.
just beneath the surface,
making no sound.
Drawing no attention to yourself.
The thief in the night
takes back her freedom
and leaves me in my chains.

Blurred Lines

You're never coming back,
and you're never going to leave.
One of those things is about you.
The other is about me.
Which is which?

Oh Really?

I forgot to breathe.
Time stood still.
The earth stopped moving.
Stars that burnt out millions of years ago
picked this second to become
invisible.
The moon aligned with the sun and froze.
The ice caps melted, yet nothing flooded.
Long dead climbers woke from there frozen slumber and
scaled down Everest;
strolled into a future without the five dollars required for a ten
cent cup of coffee.
Dogs and cats started bal room dancing, together.
Women have made peace with spiders,
and men have stopped playing fantasy football.
Tomatoes have decided to grow on trees, parsnips on vines,
and peaches as a root.
And that's what happened the last time I admitted I was wrong.

Carceral

Can you break the chains?
Achilles rides at dawn.
Raiding like a man possessed.
Contempt will drive him on.
Exodus is your only hope.
Regality buys no quarter.
Achilles storms the walls and takes your queen.
Laying you out, piece by piece before her.

Speak

Sometimes the things we say
aren't worth saying.
Sometimes the things we don't say
could charge a thousand lives,
or at least one.
Speak.

Shadow of Grace

I have been counting the minutes, the hours
and the days
since we last spoke.

I remember every dream you were in,
the feel of your flesh under my hand.
The taste of your mouth and the way you looked at me,
like it was the last time we would ever stand in front of the other.

What gifted profits your eyes are.
This is the hill you gave me to die on. You said I don't have to.
I say I do.

I'm almost weak enough to surrender,
almost strong enough to fight.
I'm lost enough to cry out and proud enough to remain silent.
I am twisted.
I need a season of renewal.
I need a trip to the field.
I need dandelions and dogs.
I need refuge in a shadow of grace.

Even Grace has a Price

His passions were ignited later in his life, and he pursued them with the vigor of a hunter. When not actively engaging, he contemplated the pursuit. His every waking moment was a study in how perfection may be achieved, because he knew his time was limited and he came to the table late. Where his life led: the desert, the mountains, the plains, the ocean, the arctic, euphoria, confinement, illness,
misery or the death bed; he would sojourn.

He would embrace his citizenship, and pursue his passions ardently, never once considering the labels he had been assigned on account of his obsessions, his tunnel vision. His very soul was invested in the execution of his art, and he'd be dammed if he'd let a handful of spaghetti-stained church deacons label him into dormancy.

Grace must be sought, sometimes with malice. Let the spaghetti stains try to take his brushes. Maybe they thought he was Don Quixote. Maybe he was. They still weren't getting his brushes.

Stand

We make our declarations.
Oh! How we declare.
We swear off this.
We swear off that.
Proclamations
born of despair.

Tectonic Plates

(i know Virginia, it's not a sonnet)

You've got me thinking
our hands may never touch.
And the words we exchange
may never be uttered casually
across a table,
with eye contact and tell-tale
expressions of affection.

But that doesn't mean our souls
didn't collide in a perfect storm
of union,
when the very first of your words
to me
leapt off the page
and revealed my own heart
in another.

Different faces, cast on the same coin.

You are worth more to me
than all the contents
of all the locked boxes
in all the shipwrecks
in all the seas.
My side of the coin would be morosely empty
without you.

Close your eyes,
reach out
and take my hand.
Distance is no match for faith.
Walls cannot stand
against will.

I will trip through your existence.

The breeze on my face
reveals
you in the shadows,
breathing life into lazy sonnets.
Breathing life into empty words.
Breathing
to show why, and how to live.
Why and how to court joy.

Little Minutes Equal Lifelong Journeys

I have a feeling that things are about to change.
Life ever after maybe wonderful and strange.

I'm seeing things a bit clearer,
holding all a bit dearer.
And not loathing so much the man in the mirror.

I'm standing on solid ground
dying to tear the walls down.

I want to chase you and catch you and make you my
companion and friend.
I want to know you and show you that I can be there until
the end.

Setting out for destinations uncharted.
It's not really all that hard to get started.
Just give me your hand and we'll take that
first little step.

We've been together for eons and oodles of time.
Life became nectarous when I became yours
and you became mine.
My words were sweeter than honey,
your presence, more precious than gold.
In a world with and without money,
our love was apparent and bold.

Now, I am dying on solid ground,
Thankful for having allowed those walls to be torn down.

I want to chase you
and catch you,
but this is the end for me.
I'm setting out for destinations uncharted
and you must set me free.

Let go of my hand love,
so I can take that last little step.
It was wonderful and strange
and I'm proud of the leap we leapt.

Be What You Need to Be

Well, I heard you woke up this morning
to find a monkey on your back.
Certainly, it's not a foreign feeling,
just another primate that fought its way
out of the sack.

Another one of your insecurities
riding you to the ground.
Pulling your hair
and spurring your ribs
as it turns your life around.

And are you the one
that can't help but push
when the sign clearly says to pull?
Is it hard for you
to take a cue,
or are you the wolf in sheep's wool?

Running up the down escalator.
Coming in through the outdoor.
Wearing those nasty boots in the house
and leaving your big muddy tracks on the floor.

Are you one of the people
who wake up every morning
dreading what they're about to do?
Would you drag your tongue through
broken glass to escape
a day in this zoo?

And are you with the people
who stand in line
wishing they were anywhere else
but here?
Can you stand boldly
against Father Time?
Can you face him without any fear?

The mirror won't show you what you want
and time won't take a break.
Should you throw your hands up in the air
and eat another slice of cake?

Or maybe you should get your first tattoo
that says born to spread my wings.
It doesn't matter what you do
to anyone but you.
Your actions are a maintenance thing.

So, eat the cake and pierce the skin
if that's what gets you off.
Life is short in a long sort of way.
Fight for your place at the trough!

Forgive yourself for the mistakes
you've made.
Make a thousand more.
Walk thin ice and live your life.
You're a tiger, guarding its kill.
Teach yourself to roar!

Love what you love
with passion.
Love what moves you
till you draw your final
breath.

Love who you love
without reason.
Love who you love boldly.
Enwreathe them in your love
till death.

And play the game to win,
whatever that means for you.
Use every pawn at your disposal.
Be passionate.
Be ruthless.
Be true.
Fear not. March forward.
Be quintessentially you.

Under the Mushroom

When I talk to you
the world seems so much larger.
I'm standing under a mushroom
looking out.
Seeing everything for the first time.

Through the soft moss
that I want to lay with you in,
while staring straight up
a peeling birch tree.
Obsessed with the blue sky
beyond its branches
and how the clouds compliment
the rough
and sometimes
porous paper bark.

I want to tell you all the ways you move me.
But I will let the breeze through the pine needles
tell that tale.
My mouth is otherwise engaged here,
under our mushroom.
My mouth is whispering
to another part of you
that needs every filthy word.

I need that part of you
to pull it from me.
To grab my tongue and hold it hostage.
Here, under our mushroom.

Here under our mushroom
"no" is in short supply.
Here under our mushroom
anticipation seeps through our pores.
Here under our mushroom
You're gonna get everything you want,
but it's coming slow,
and deliberate.

When the words escape my lips
and find you,
will you say them with me?
Or will you fill my mouth
with a new language and
brush my lips with a new tongue,
here under our mushroom, under a baby blue sky?
Eyes closed, and a hand on each side of my face,
pushing and pulling and saying filthy things.
Here under our mushroom.

3800 Miles

His joints
they're all a aching.
His throat
feels like broken glass.
If he had known this day
would last so long,
he surely would have passed.

And he's a stranger
in a strange land. The California plains.
There's no rest, no relief,
no remedy for his aches and pains.

He wants to crawl under the covers,
just pull them over his head.
Utterly alone in this shithole world.
He'd be fine
if they left him for dead.

But, When the muse
she comes a knocking,
you better
let her in.
She ain't one to stand for mocking,
and you know she's your only friend.

So, here you are around Bakersfield.
Steel wool where your esophagus
should be.
Eyelids so heavy
and talking to yourself,
Not trusting everything you see.

He wants to shut it all out.
Drown out *all* the damn noise.
no dinner at the Truckers table,
no rubbing elbows with the boys.

He was never good at it anyway,
whether he was sick
or ready to run a race.
He needs no voice,
or a slap on the shoulder.
All he needs is ten hours of rest
in a warm and quiet place.

But when the muse
she comes a knocking,
You better
let her in.
She ain't one to stand for
mocking.
And you need at least one friend.

So, his mind ain't clicking like it should.
Yet she makes him say these words.
Destined as they are for the burn barrel.
Destined to never be heard.

Whatever is happening behind his eyelids
will always take a backseat.
She's getting in.
She's taking the reins.
She's turning up the heat.

Because when the muse, she comes a knocking,
You better let her in.
She ain't one to stand for mocking.
And she ain't above a little sin.

When Dawn Blooms the East Will Blush

I'm waiting,
with my eyes closed
and my heart open,
because it has room.
I am waiting in my field, vulnerable.
Blissfully unaware.
Arms and legs, outstretched. Inviting.

I'm waiting for dawn,
and the promise of a new day.
New strength.
New hope.
New energy.
New love.

I'm waiting for dawn in my field.
I'm waiting for you.
I will make you a canvas and stroke you in wildflower.

I'm waiting for dawn to bathe me in light,
to open my eyes,
to feed a soul,
to fill a heart.
To stand shoeless in the mud with me,
to point our faces to Heaven,
mouths wide open and catching raindrops.

There is no hurt,
no thirst,
no hunger,
no intense lonely longing,
no isolation,
no deprivation,
no dark, dark corners in the light of dawn.

When dawn brings the tide, the rocks rejoice.
When dawn brings the light, the dark steps back.
When dawn brings a voice, it is a blanket that leaves nothing
uncovered.

Step towards dawn.
Rely on the honest light she brings.
And if she brings the rain,
strip down before her as the tendrils of water wash away the
crusty residual, resentment.
Like rivulets moving driftwood.

Dry in the light of dawn.
Be warm in the light of dawn.
Heal in the light of dawn.

Offer up your flesh to the dawn,
a canvas in a field, stroked by wildflowers,
and bearing a masterpiece.

The muse works through you as you work through it.
Let every morning be your muse.
Embrace Dawn every day.

Watch as she chooses her shades from the palette
and paints broad, easy,
generous strokes across your life.
Not because you were somehow worthy
of this gift.
But because
somehow, someway,
you brought color to the light dawn wields
and she noticed,
and she has claimed you.

You're a houseplant that had no hope,
brown and withering.
Dawn turned the soil
and exposed your roots.
Dawn brought the light
and led the rain.
She splinted your shoots and gave you the prime spot by the
glass.
Dawn knows the color in you her light will bring,
and the fruit you will bear, and she is patient.
She waits for your promise to shine.
And shine it will, in the light of dawn,
you happy, lucky accident.

Muleshoe, Texas and Dustbowl Musings

The iron bell is tolling.
It makes a plaintive sound.
I know not where I'm going and
I will not stay around.

The wind was blowing fierce today.
Muleshoe was hardly seen.
Cotton and dust.
Pivots and rust.
A drifter, haggard and lean.
A carpet bag with essentials.
One thumb up in the air.
Dancing between the tumbleweeds,
the soil finds his hair.

The winter wheat sways in
turbulent winds.
It is witness to the rage.
A billboard face and crime scene tape
pass like an unread page.
Will Mother Nature be assuaged?

I can't see down the road too far,
the blacktop is old and cracked.
I could be
in the last century,
but the GPS brings me back.

Jalopies in front yards.
Horses and longhorns in the field.
Feedlot smells and tolling bells and
spines of Damascus Steel.

I see their world in black and white.
It's likely they do too.
Regionalists,
true to a fault.
The citizens of Muleshoe.

I see the rust.
The soil, black as night,
and derricks pumping up and down.
They feed the soil with their blood.
Their home is hallowed ground.

It ain't that much to look at but,
it's damn sure hallowed ground.

Oaths That Can't be Kept

I
would die
a thousand deaths
to free you from your chains.
And I
would die
a thousand more
to wash away what stains.
And I
would eat
my beating heart
to steal your aches and pains.

And I
would break the
doors of heaven
to make you feel again.

So,
move that strand of
hair form your face and
look me in the eye.

My
Intent is evident,
and as conspicuous as the sky.

Self-Loathing and the Verbose Villain

How do I wring solace from this inkwell?
This quill, this mutinous pen vexes me.
The white bull mocks me.
When all the sentiments have been expressed,
in all the unique and
all the peculiar ways they could be.
I am a thief, taking from here and from there and
building my own beast.
When all the musical notes have been played in
all the combinations,
all the variations.
When an original thought is harder to grasp than a star,
a rainbow,
or an accident of light.
When you have nothing interesting to say because
it's all been said,
how do I tell you how I feel?
And why would I?
"Because you are dull, my *boy*." whispers the Unquiet Mind.
"Boring, witless beyond reason. Original thoughts escape you.
You string together words in a mish mash fashion.
Choosing them for how they sound against a background and
not as your conveyor of feeling.
They are the echo of an axe landing on a log in the neighbor's
yard three houses down.
They are the mirror you preen in.
Yet you continue to seek your validation in whatever gutter,
(Look at me! Hear me! Love me! THIS wordy motherfucker!)
you may find it in.

The conventional channels for attention have failed you.
The enemies you cling to.
The traitors that sing to you.
Classically, they kiss you.
Astonishingly, you kiss them back and
you say...
something that had been said before, many times over by
better men and women than you.
Only after having masked it with your thesaurus.
Something quite forgettable.
Something irretrievable.
Something inconceivable. Something.
What would you be in a world without words?
Just another thing that feeds?
A belly?
An ego?
A soul?
A libido?
A word to the wise is lacking.
A word to the wise we are tracking.
What word or two has gotten in you?
Whose word do you find yourself backing?
How easily distracted.
Focus. What do you want to say?"

It must be confusing how you loathe and love yourself at the
same time." the unquiet mind whispers in your ear.

The Pitcher Plant Stands Not Alone

Nomadic Stranger.
I travel unencumbered.
Galvanized, unconcerned with the need that surrounds me.
I am apathetic. I am teflon.
Callous as a pitcher plant. Watching,
waiting for the trap to spring.
Waiting for the victim to slide down the pitfall.
To dissolve in the sweet nectar that was the lure.
Remorseless.
Assigning the sacrifice blame.
"Should you not?" it whispers from within.
"After all, you clawed your way out. Who threw you a line?"
I hate that unquiet fiend.
The louder it gets the farther I fly,
the less I care,
the quieter I become.
I am the nomadic stranger,
giving the unquiet mind a wide berth
and a despotic autonomy,
and fleeing the company of the real world.
My collar pulled up,
my hat pulled down, averting my eyes.
Fearful that the world will see right through me.
Yet hoping to achieve a state of opacity equal to zero.
The pitcher plant stands not alone.
I am the things in me that I loathe,
and I fear the things in others that I love.

Want Confliction

I want what I can't have,
what doesn't want me back.
What is far out of my reach and what would step away, out of
my grasp.
I want what I don't need.
What I can live without.
What makes no difference in my life.
I want what amounts to
little grains of sand in the picnic basket,
the grit against the soft white bread.
I want you even though I know you look right through me.
I have assigned you status in my heart.
To you, I am as significant as a can opener.
Muscle memory insists that I reach for you,
even though the mind remembers someone else.
The heart doesn't care.
My mind knows that you are just my heart's attempt to
replace another soul that was indifferent to me; it knows,
muscle memory doesn't care,
it just needs a job to give the arms.
The mind is outnumbered.
Desire is a masked sociopath setting up dominoes and
knocking them over.
The weak watch the parade.
Let muscle memory win one every now and then, but
put that heart in a box and don't let it out until
a soul that lends light to your landscape
peeks up over the horizon.

This is Going to get Ugly

My ghosts all come to haunt me when
I've found a place of rest.
My fears attempt to strangle me the
second I've caught my breath.
My sheepishness is evident in all I say or do.
I am no more deliberate than a stranger passing through.
I am aware of the effect my apprehensions have on me.
And I alone must slay those beasts to set my spirit free.
I must cast the light that drives those shadows out.
And I will crush my ancient adversary, the Harbinger of Doubt.
But this act cannot be done without uneasiness, angst, or fear.
To dispatch this corrival, I must reject
my tormentor from the mirror.
The Unquiet Mind gently snickers, "Look
at you with the pieces laid about.
What kind of life do you think you'll
have when you've cast me out?
I've been your constant companion
from the cradle till the now.
You're going nowhere without me, *boy*.
No way, nowhere, no how."

Exodus from You

I could never have walked away from what you offered me.
My mind was made for me before the stars decided to shine.
You were the narrow path. I was the ox.
The burden bearing beast on a road that could not support it.
You were unassuming and demure in the beginning.
But you taught yourself to love the whip,
and the whip to love the flesh.
And you taught the flesh to peel before you.
To peel *for* you.
For your pleasure.
For your amusement.
At your whim.
For a few fleeting seconds of satisfaction,
to appease the sadist within you.
And appeased you were.
Every welt, a grin.
Every moan raising the hair on your arms.
Every shriek causing your lips to quiver.
Every bruise making you wet.
Every drop of blood compelling you to drop your free hand to
the source of the wetness and apply the pressure you crave,
all while still plying the whip.
You are who you are because,
I am someone else.
Someone who felt.
Someone who loved.
Someone willing to ignore warning signs and common sense.
A beast in a hallway between dining rooms.
A trader of sweet cream for tepid water.

For you.
You, who were so accustomed to reward, you ceased to
appreciate the sacrifice.
Never for you.
Never again.
My blood, sweat and tears.
My ups and downs.
My pleasure and pain.
My willingness to throw myself on your alter.
Or my willingness to ignore the fact that
someone who wanted to hold the reins,
crack the whip and
steer the cart,
thought it beneath them to
feed and groom the beast.
You were only ever willing to apply the yoke.
My pleasure and pain are no onger here for your amusement.
Not another ounce of life shed for you.
I am the beast, biding its time, waiting to see you fall.

A Servant Evolves

I taste the day between my lips.
It has the flavor of isolation and parking lot dust.

I would trade it for a bucket of crayfish and beer.
For conversation and eye contact.
But not with a random, talkative stranger.
I am trying.
You can tell.
But I don't know if I have it in me.

Surrender may be my sanctuary.
What have I to surrender anyway?
I have no army.
I have no will.

All the best pieces of me have already been taken or exploited.
Or sold.
My bones have been picked clean.
What is left is hardly desirable as spoils.
What is left is more accurately,
ruins.

What remains of my days?
Sanctuary?
It is a deceptive term.
Sanctuary is there, but at what cost?
No!

What remains for me is what has always been.
The role I was always groomed for.
With every path that was chosen for me and
with every path I chose.
With every reinforcing lash of the
tongue
and every stroke of the lash,
service is my sanctuary.

It is dull and crusted, my sanctuary.
Bland and incandescent.
I exist in a place where colors run.
The thorn on the rose, more brilliant and exalted than the
petals.
With more to say than the bloom.

I am an exile from polite company and tramps.
Too filthy for one,
too clean for the other.
Always a step behind in every conversation.
The awkward, gawky stepchild.
The least interesting thing in a room full of bureaucrats.

So, I hide in the shadows of service.
I seek and find my sanctuary in obscurity.
Longing for a day to draw attention to myself and
terrified of the notion.

Quietly,
I see the things you do.
They excite and repulse me here in the shadows where I hide.
Where I watch.

I hear the things you tell each other
when you don't know I am there,
lurking.
The man with the piano was right,
tis better to laugh with the many
than to cry with the few.
But I can't even do this.

So, I drift from
shadow to shadow
and field to field.
I am Tom Joad with no conviction.
In a world full of Tom Joads with
no moral fiber.

More comfortable in the dust of a parking lot
thinking about beer and crayfish
than sitting in a casino on a barstool
in the air conditioning
on this Easter Sunday,
drinking beer
and eating crayfish.

I am an owl in a rotting oak,
waiting for the mice to scurry.
I'm a grifter, swapping lies,
searching for favor to curry.

I am the breeze,
calming your heart,
blowing away your worries.
And, I am the one who knocks.
Executioner, judge, and jury.

Taste this parking lot.
This prairie, this field on my lips.
Touch my heart and take my hand; lead me home.
I no longer have a desire to serve.
It is my intention
to consume.

Golden Hours

An empty field am I.
Ancient, yet still so much potential.
How to harness it? Your guess is as good as mine.
I'm a shorn cornfield.
Golden in the golden hours of spring.
The pivot hasn't moved in ages.
And when it does,
It goes nowhere.
It grinds its gears.
Moving in circles.
Re-visiting the starting line, over and over.
But, it serves, it nourishes. Then, it sleeps.
The texture of the cottonwoods. The lines in my face.
So similar, so earned.
But not sought.

The branches bare,
like my soul. But not for long.
The bordering stream, the budding season.
The sun.
The ancient sun, somehow new (It should teach me that
trick.)
and driving potential, driving growth.
Another opportunity to shed the stale. To begin anew.
To face one's own self.
To grow,
in a new season like I know I can,
even if the past isn't all that encouraging.
Spread your wings and fly!

Spin your webs you industrious Gods!
You congregation of thoughtful geniuses!
Shake off the past, take a scalpel to the present and prune
I say!!
Cut away the parasitical branches.
Remember the lessons of last year.
Weed out the suckers.

There is no time to dwell on the past.
And I have not what it takes to repeat it.
Take my hand, we'll spin our webs together.
Let us spin in the golden hours.
Let us whisper our personal conspiracies and
wallow in the act of goal-oriented execution.
We shall create.
And we shall bathe in the glory of our creation,
here
in the golden fields, in the golden hours.
In our golden hearts.

Never My Blood. Never Less Than My Brother. Always My Heart

At Last.
Contentment settles in.
You're in a peaceful state of mind.
Your breaths are long and easy.
And for the moment,
the world is not unkind.

I never cared to be the first in line.
I never needed to occupy the inner circle.
I never needed to be more important than I was,
until I did.

I just needed a direction,
something to focus on,
a caravan to join.
A destination to reach for,
with like-minded fools
and like-minded conspirators.
Brothers in arms.
Juggling bowling pins and
hiding behind our face paint.
There is sanctuary in a mask.

I needed a mountain to climb.
Slow and meticulous the ascent.
Some stop to smell the roses,
I needed to see the bodies of those that went before me.

Their limbs, twisted in odd directions,
half buried in the ice and snow.
Humorous, peaceful grins on their frozen faces.
I check their pockets for anything useful.
A book of matches?
A coin?
A clue?

In my dreams I can fly.
I catch currents and run with them.
Time marches persistently, monotonously forward.
It is a Roman Legion,
marching through the desert in search of an enemy
that gasps for water,
as I watch from above.

Some will tell you,
time's only objective is to convert that
which is young
to that which is old.

I believe that time
is the distance that the wounded
put between their heart,
and the heart that wounded them.

Time is the republic that I give my
melancholy dominion over.
There are no term limits in this district.

Time is a unit of measurement.
"The fish had to be huge, it took me *forever* to reel it in. Too
bad it slipped the hook."

Time is the carrot and the stick.
It is the tonic that heals,
and the cancer that kills.
Time is limited for you and
endless for the stars.
Time and distance.
Time and distance.

Time and distance are formidable barriers to love,
to life,
to peace and peace of mind.

But as great as they are and
as much as they have separated me
from my caravan,
my conspirators,
time and distance will *never* erode
the esteem and affection
I have always borne for you my brothers.
My brothers in arms.

Anchored

All our defining little minutes laid out before us.

A tablecloth, stained.
Rose petal rubbed between thumb and index finger.
The worry you carry uselessly.

Weighing you down
Weighing you down

Velvet gloves on naked skin.
Held accountable for every sin.
Hide your eyes from the dreadful past.
Pay your penance, pay it fast.
It's weighing you down.
It's weighing you down.

I'm standing here,
in my corner.
Eyes shut tight and dreading the judgement to come.
But I stand in fear of the wrong jurists.
I know it.

My weakness for
the opinions of others.
The renown I achieve.

Smoke in the wind.
Smoke in the wind.

I am a slave to
the slightest recognition.
And I crave it,
like the junkie craves the needle.

Stick me.

I am the veiny, rust colored maple leaf,
waiting for mother nature
to recycle me.

And it's weighing me down.
weighing me down.

I am the seed,
carried by the bird.
Will I bloom where it plants me?

Back me into the corner.
Will the animal appear?
Or am I the good dog?

Feed me.

I am the stray,
the beautiful loser,
the dividing line.
I stand before the point of no return,
uneasy with the decision before me,
so, I never make one.

And it's weighing me down.
weighing down.

I am the one who waits.
I waited for the stars to align.
I waited for the
promise that never materialized.
And I waited for you to touch me.
How is it that you held my heart so tightly in your hand
without ever having to have touched me?
That, is a trick you shall have to teach me,
because the not knowing...
is weighing down.

No Other Way No Way as Way

The soul turns around as
you stand in place.
Thoughts weigh heavy on you both.
The miles are hard on your heels and
Your shoes collect pebbles.

How long will you continue to walk
before you slip them off,
one at a time,
dancing on one foot
and then the other.
Turning the shoes upside down and
watching the small, smooth stones
tumble back to earth.

Or have you grown dependent on
the impediment?
It drives you.
(Mad?)
Some people *need* the bitter to make the meal palatable.
They revel in the struggle.
They bloom in the storm.
Are you a storm bloomer?
God, I hope so.
Let us tempt the lightning!
Let us try the flood!
I don't want to die,
but I would rather expire
than to have failed
to live.

Lady Liberty Bends Over

When the darkness comes to claim you.
When the demons come to prey.
When the hope is lost within you. When
it seems you've lost your way.
When the shit piles up upon you, and
your back is against the wall.
When foe and friend surround you,
both eager to watch you fall.

When the greasy dirt builds under your nails
with nary a splinter to dig it out.
When you've nothing left with which to
protest, not even the voice to shout.
When you've had enough of the treachery
of those that wish to harm.
When manufactured camaraderie was
never meant to save the farm.

When a seven-thousand-dollar suit
wants to tell you how to live.
Claiming to respect those worn-out knees
while scoffing at what you give.
When they price you out of business.
When they take away your land.
When their objective has nearly been
reached and Armageddon is at hand.

Goodbye middle class. Hello peasantry!
Meet the new boss in all her glory.
Call her Aristocracy.
We put that little bitch in place but we can't remember how.
She has us marching to her drum, marching here and now.

She divided us with media. Race. Abortion. Guns and Fuel.
Never personally having fired a shot
while taking this nation of fools.

She'll take it cause you won't stand together,
won't vote with half a brain.
We allow ourselves to be divided, the fools revere their chains.
She encourages you to vote security
and toss freedom to the side.
Those who do are deserving of neither
and the rest of us must rise.

More or Less

I make my observations with my eyes wide shut.
You were thoroughly vetted if you made the cut.
You were judged against... I'm not sure what.
You probably want to hold off on that winner's strut.

I've been known to hide and self-deprecate.
My relationship with the mirror is less love than hate.
But the second *You* come around here just to denigrate,
I'll kick your ass so hard it's gonna change your gait.

Why don't you tell me again
how less is more.
How you've cleared that
path for me up to Heaven's door.

An ego that large ought
to make a back real sore.
I've heard everything you're saying,
maybe less is more.

We never did agree on the color of
a burnt orange sky.
You always claimed the high ground yet,
I never knew why.
You went away and left me quite high and dry.
Shit bird!
If I say I haven't missed you then you know it's a lie.

"Hey Boy!" me all day. Go ahead.
Gimmie what you got.
I may be somewhat meek,
but I'll drop you on the spot.
And I won't pack the truth in heavy syrup to
ease your fragile mind.
Anything less than candor is a
waste of my time.

Why don't you tell me again
how less is more.
How you've cleared that
path for me up to Heaven's door.
An ego that large
ought to make a back real sore.
I've heard everything you're saying,
maybe less is more.

Clay Pots are Afterthoughts

You just need to start.
Pick a direction and go.
There is only the journey for now.

Under and over
but never around.
Never around.
Always through,
always you.

Swim the streams.
Fall the trees.
Cross the desert.
And occasionally, look at the midnight sky.

Hang your hopes on a star or two,
and stand like a fool in the pouring rain.
Face up.
Mouth open.
Arms extended.
You are a pauper and a God in the same breath,
in a place where it is desirable to be both.

Grab hands of soil, black as onyx and put it in your pockets,
so you'll have something to grow your dreams in
when you have decided to hallow your ground.

Dreams grown in clay pots.
Nourished by experience, temerity, patients and
a whole lot of star gazing and rain dancing.
Speak to the dreams in your clay pots.
Live, you little bastards! I need you!

It's Funny when that Happens

Were my motives ever pure?
Or, did I take you just for the having,
for the wanting?

Did I take you for the pleasure,
for the little minute of bliss?

Did I misunderstand the rules?
Did I stay too long?
Did the tables turn?

Was it you who was interested in
the little minute?
Did you evolve the second I blinked?
Did I?

Was I supposed to toe the line,
adhere to the parameters of
the understanding
when it dawned on me
that you are the pearl?

Was I supposed to pretend that you were not?
How could I have taken my pleasure and
walked away from you?

The tables turned.
I was the hunter, and now it is you.
I am the prey.
Willing to be caught, had and rejected
by the hunter.

The Bird that's Thrown from the Nest Isn't Supposed to Live

Innocence.
A destination forgotten,
It's no longer on the map in
my world.
Guilt is the destination, or some outpost of it.
Shame is the price of the ticket.

Shame is my currency.
Guilt, my country, and I am patriotic to her.
No amount of drugs, alcohol or sex can separate me
from my flag.
My programming was achieved expertly.
I am painfully aware that nothing I ever do will have been
worth doing.

Flowers in bloom
wilt in my shadow.
I see pawns like myself,
ignorant.
Blissfully unaware of
just how insignificant their toil is.
Yet they spend their weekends eating pecan pie,
drinking average bourbon
and fucking blissfully.

What a relief for them,
unencumbered by the doubt that hounds me.
Un-assaulted by the guilt I feel after

having knocked off a seventy-hour week and
knowing those efforts to be feeble, unworthy.
Not hounded by the shame of knowing
that no matter what you do your
success will be attributed to someone else,
while your failures are the children
you were always told
you would produce.

On my shoulders I carry monuments to my own ineptitude,
looking for a place to plant them.
I would love to plant them right on top of those
who gave them to me.
But that would be viewed as ungrateful,
and Heaven knows
we should delight in every gift.
Does not the burning bag of dog shit provide light?
Then what are you complaining about?
You're the one who stepped in it,
now clean up your mess.

Walk with me my brothers.
the whipping post is ours.
Let's bare our backs in the sun
and receive with joy our scars.

The scars we get for believing
our minds are our own.
Tongue separates rib from flesh
to drive the counterpoint home.

Rejuvenate the Loner Transient

It was a day.
It was a gift.
It was a reminder and
a ringing of the bell.

It was time as precious as oxygen.
An event for the senses.
A temporary rejection of life lived on autopilot.

I sat across from you and consumed your every utterance,
your every gesture.
Every movement of your eyes.
The rising and falling of your chest as
you breathed the easy breaths of
the assured and displayed the magnanimity
of a summer breeze.

I consumed you.
And you allowed it to be so.
You suffered clumsy attempts at humor,
and brevity of thought with grace.

The other night, you were a garden feeding the malnourished.
A voice.
A palm on the flesh.
A smile.
A secret whispered in one's ear.

You were a lifeline
weaving a tapestry of care.
A blanket providing comfort.
I am grateful.

The Beckoned

When I beckon sin
she comes.
Sin's own digits
hollow out the fjord.
The sea below slapping the walls.
Keeping them moist.,
glistening
and satiated.
I am the tide beckoning sin.
I move at the whim of the moon.
She beckons.
I move.
No rejection.
Celestial bodies slide together,
writhing in breathless anticipation.
Their reflection dancing across the sea below,
bouncing merrily
off the glistening walls.
Vessel drifting to the point where
the walls are joined and
the fjord is realized.
Offering a full mouth kiss
where pressure invites itself to dinner,
devours everything that is offered and
licks the plate clean.

One day, standing at the fjord, you beckon sin.
One day, standing at the fjord, sin beckons you.

Pulling the Threads at my Seams

No.
No is the wall constructed in frustration.
No is the wall I cannot scale.
No is the wall that primes my hesitation.
No is the wall where sum and substance are unveiled.

Dark
Dark is the void that drives a man to unreason.
Dark is the need that bends him low.
Dark is the mind sequestered for a season.
Dark are the seeds the unrestrained then sow.

Will
Will is the pressure you exert over me.
Will is the resistance I bring to bear on you.
Will is the rock holding back the angry sea.
Will sees the many bow before the few.

Lace
Lace is a delicate promise on the wind.
Lace is the fabric most likely to deceive.
Lace is a whisper, a hint of things to come.
Lace is the fiction we allow ourselves to believe.

Mercy
Mercy is what I beg of you daily.
Mercy is the weak leading the frail.
Mercy is tainted ground granted gaily.
Mercy is the wall on which your mama wails.

Hiding.
Hiding in plain sight, the chameleon checks his watch.
Hiding in the weeds the leach waits for flesh.
Hiding my intentions in a wrinkled, brown paper sack.
Hiding is difficult for the grandiose character, enmeshed.

Where is This?

At what lies beneath the linens
so early in the morn.
Eyes move across
with privilege
at so divine a form.
It stirs the soul within you
to its very core.

Yes!
The Ceiling
and windows.
Yes!
The kitchen nook.
Yes!
The bats in my belfry
perusing ancient books.

Indeed, there is a home,
behind that magic door.
The worthy few
adored by you
will tread upon its floor.

"Does it lead to Oz or Narnia?",
the transient wonders now.
Ruling lions
and flying monkeys,
or dancing pigs and cows.

None of these things
will impede
his desire to gaze on you.
To caress that skin
with the palm
of his hand
to bathe
in the peace imbued.

Doyenne

She catches all my little gestures.
My idiosyncrasies.
She's a calm, cool voice of reason.
A moment of pause,
the breeze that brings relief as the sun sets
and casts the shadows that
coax the day into an easy and comfortable slumber.

Doyenne is smooth as silk
as she claims my threadbare soul.
The touch of her palm on my arm bleeds me of
my bewilderment.
A sideway glance,
a word
and a half sardonic little smile drives the rage
from the textures inside that rage clings to,
and replaces it with an easy blanket of serenity.

I have never been hungry
in her presence.
And I can't decide if she is
a servant, savior,
or saint.

But, sometimes I wonder what would happen if
I offered her my throat.
Because I was always gracious
to the chickens
in an easy and reassuring way,
till I brought the hatchet down.
Bring the hatchet down.
Bring the hatchet down.

Wipe away the blood and feathers from
the walls of the slaughter room.
Put an edge on that blade.
Get the block in place,
and beckon Dcyenne with the promise
of a pulsing vein.

Because I Said So

"What is your name child?"
"Doyenne."
"Doyenne?"
"Yes."
"Doyenne of what?"
"What?"
"What are you Doyenne of?"
"I said I am Doyenne, not the doyenne,
it is my name, not a designation."
"That doesn't satisfy me child. How did you get this name?"
"My father gave it to me."
"And *he* knew you to be Doyenne?"
"He liked the sound of it, it was almost pretty. He liked the
meaning, he thought I might grow into it."
"So, how are you Doyenne?"
(long pause)

"I am Doyenne because my father named me so. In a room
full of nurses, I am Doyenne and maybe one day, I will be the
doyenne. Under a bridge with the homeless, I am Doyenne.
Running a cash register or selling life insurance, I am Doyenne.
Owner of a restaurant, or employee in the kitchen, or one of
the waitresses, I am Doyenne. Working with horses in a barn or
performing criminal miracles as a certified public accountant,
I am Doyenne. White collar or blue, beckoning sin, servicing
saints or playing hearts with the emotionally incarcerated, I am
now and always will be Doyenne. One day, I may even be the
doyenne.".

"But for now, I say,
Rose is not a rose,
unless you're Gertrude Stein.
Triple down in my classroom,
I will see you ride the pine."
(lorg pause)
"What?"
Doyenne walks away with a smile.

Walk Away Blue, Chance and Triggers

I lost my mind somewhere down the line.
It flew away and is flying to this day.
I can't keep track, don't know if it's coming back.

It's a long, long road.

Dogs and flowers bring me to my knees.
They have the power to grant me joy, to put my mind at ease.
Nothing is sour among the trees.

I've been triggered. I saw you yesterday.
I had figured I was over it in every way.
But, these feelings lingered. God,
I hope they are not here to stay.
And it's a long, long road.

With all these feelings running round, I ask myself,
"are my feet firmly on the ground?".
I have to say no, in every way.
But I take it day by day, and I just go on.

It's a long, long road.

I'll get my mind back eventually. My feet will find the ground.
I'll get up off my knees.
And I will live you down.

The living I do without you will make the living
we did together
seem so very grey.
And I will thank God profusely, thank him you did not stay.
It will be over in every conceivable way.

But for now, you are the wind,
that pushes the tumbleweed again and again.
And it's a long, long road.

Feeling Moon Dancy

We are well into another Autumn,
and I love to hear the waves
break on the shore.
The rocks are sanctuary from
top to bottom.
When I'm here I forget
I'm not exactly a young man anymore.

The October leaves,
they are a showing.
The red, orange and golds.
Oh! how vibrant they bleed.
So brilliant in their oaks
and maples.
Such a sight on which the eyes may feed.
Enchanted nights,
so crisp and cool,
Moon shines her light while
Scarecrow plays the barnyard fool.

Woodsmoke
Compost and
apple pie.
Eell jars,
hay bales and
eerie, haunted skies.

Take the other seasons, you can have them all.
I'll take the briny, biting, icy autumn coastline
with its rosehips and sea spray,
a glass of warm cider
and New England in the fall.

The Unquiet Mind in a Rare Moment of Something Less than Cruelty

There's a symphony
in my head,
annoying all my friends.
The crescendo never ends.

Till I'm dead.
Till I'm dead.

I been hearing it for years,
this ringing in my ears.

Evoking fear.
stoking fear.
Put your jimmie foot forward.
Over here.
Over here.

We got some rhythm brought by strings,
a skanky writhing thing.
Lay it down over brass,
add some words and
make them crass.

There's a pulse moving through
this untenanted avenue
where we play the blues.
That color to imbue.

A day we will not rue.
A day we will not rue.

Take it on the chin.
That beat has you locked in.
Shake your ass in sin.

Delicious grin.
Delicious grin.

Now you just can't stop.
Is it rock or is it pop?
Hit the bottom, hit the top.
Grab a mop.
Do the Hop.

Swing the doors wide.
No longer will you hide.
On the rhythm you will ride.
Pick a side.
Pick a side.

Shifting Tides

She never sleeps.

Have you ever sat on the shoreline to
listen to the waves come home?
Thrilling the rocks with tales
of their distant travels.

Harbor seals bark their approval,
while the seagulls squeal with delight.
Your eyes are closed, and you chin turned up
because your soul has taken flight.

The sea spray hits me in the face and
I taste the salt in the air.
It gets under my skin and
asks where I've been and
I say, "I haven't been anywhere."

This is *my* seething ocean and
I hate it when I go away.
I was always me or
what they told me to be.
I will tread the water anywhere,
everyday.

Her roar is a comfort to me and
I live in the shadow of her jealousy.
She wants me like no other has.
She sees what no other sees.

I am a child of the Atlantic.
But I am a bastard in my own hometown.
You won't find me rubbing too many elbows
because I *need* those ocean sounds.

I need the starfish in the pools and
the seaweed on the rocks.
The coming and going of her tide
is my body clock.

I need the "fizz" of the ocean foam.
And no mere woman shall I seek.
I want a lithe and scaly love.
I want a mermaid from the deep.

So, I stand here at the edge,
after months of being
away.
Tempted to relieve this world,
to sacrifice,
to keep the hounds at bay.

The Atlantic.
She never sleeps.
I am hers and when she calls,
I will go with nary a peep.

But,
I want to arouse in her the storm,
I want to take my pleasure in her sight,
I want to provoke her envy, excite her fervor and
watch her rage all night.

Rain down on me in cold drops of anger, wild!
Scrub away my seditious ways!
Beat me meek and mild!

Show me that you want me and
I will do what you want me to,
looking down in contrition when
I fill my lungs for you.

Add my name to the taken.
I shall respond to the roll call of history.
I am a child of the Atlantic.
I crave her kiss,
and the intrigue of a watery end
shrouded in mystery.

Cemetery Road Never Scared Me

Distance.
Distance is my greatest adversary,
aside from that loud fiend
in my mind.

Look in the mirror and
mentally peel back the years,
the layers.
The unlaughing lines under those eyes.

The years equal distance.
An uncrossable void,
from world weary
to innocence.
Oh, but you crossed that void from innocence to world weary?
There is no way back.

Light travels
where light will.
Gravity bends light.
Does it break?

I am the rock,
eroded by the waves.
Where are the pieces of me
that have been cast aside,
carried away by the current
and forgotten by time?
I haven't forgotten them.

I haven't forgotten the faces of innocence.
I haven't forgotten that
rain can bring joy.
I haven't forgotten the
unquestionable love of a dog.
I haven't forgotten ice cream made soft
in your bowl
with the spoon,
or the community swimming pool.
I haven't forgotten playing cards in
bicycle spokes or
little league on Saturday morning.
I haven't forgotten the octogenarians
waiting on the front porch
for the paperboy,
handing him warm cookies,
the price of the paper and
his very first saunterings into adult conversation,
and a smile.

I haven't forgotten Cemetery Road.
I knew where
they buried the bodies,
and I know where they bury them today,
and why.
And it is not for the same reasons.

The Volume and the Echo.
The Voices and the Voice

Lonely and longing.
But the transient heart is an introvert.
It can't possibly live without you.
Till it finds itself painted in the corner.
Painted there with you.
Learning who you are.
Then it couldn't possibly live with you.
The reluctance is not a reflection on you.

You were never unpleasant enough to inflict myself on you
in a permanent way.
I didn't deserve you.
I knew it.

When the dance is over
and the lights come on,
and the wallflower abandons his voyeuristic endeavor and
cedes his energy,
his aura to the fugitive.
The runner,
the quiet, contemplative
cellar dweller.
The thoughtful psychopath,
trapped in a thousand mirrors.
Breaking them
one at a time,
looking for an exit.

Slave to his own
error of parallax.
Slave to the voice.
The voices, before they became one.

The volume and the echo, unbearable.
Where are the days on the baseball diamond?
Do you remember what it was like to lay in the middle of
the field, exposed to everything Earth had to offer and never
once finding a tick on your flesh as you stripped down for the
night?
Do parasites not feed on the innocent?
They're not bitter enough?
Not yet savory,
to the taste?

Avert your eyes.
It's just another mirror.
Another life.
Another you.
A you that wasn't paranoid.
A you that wasn't loathed.
A you that wasn't beaten down by shifting tides or
changing opinions.
A you, uncorrupted.
A you so damn dumb that you could assign
no sinister motive to the overtly evil.
A you that only exists in your own mind.
A you that only exists in one of the mirrors.

How do we break into *that* mirror?
How do we avoid the shards?

Hay fields and pine trees and garter snakes
in the poppies.

Horses and country roads and crisp winter mornings.

Unamused teachers and quite amused adolescent girls.

Amused and amusing.

Paper routes and Victorian houses and those elderly folks who
dwelled in them, and talked across to you, not down.

Rose hips on the coast and the waves pounding the rocks.
Gulls squawking and Cormorants preening.

Grandma giving you that smile.
How do I get back in that mirror?
Change the angle.
Ain't it heavy?

Just one more game of ping pong
with my math teacher.
One more Brunswick Times Record sacrificed to the
goat on my route.
One more first kiss.
One more toboggan ride on my feet two decades before the
snowboard was invented.

One more day! Ignorant and happy!
One more day, blissfully unaware of what
we are all painfully aware of now.

How do I get into that mirror?
If I ever break that mirror,
the volume and echo will be unbearable.

The volume and the echo. The voices and the voice.
Every mirror broken multiplies.

God help the introvert
trapped in the wrong mirror.
God help me when I look up
with a straight face
only to find my caricature
smiling manically at me.

The Ghost and Her Stones

She comes to me at night.
The one that slipped away.
She saunters in as gracefully
as she sauntered out.

She comes to me at night.
But she doesn't come to stay.

She moved me with a smile.
She beguiled me with her style,
knowing all the while
that the space between us
was more than miles.
Knowing all the while that for me,
her absence would be a trial.

But she flies in and she flies out
on the breeze.
She touches nothing but my core and
her scent lingers,
and the draft whispers her name.

I feel her breath on my neck.
And I remember her fingers
raising bumps on my flesh,
and actual words parting her lips.
Oh!
She could put words together.
And they were magic.

She spoke sentences that were
nothing less than a bridge
to contentment.
Words that bound me to her
like pages to the spine.

A word spoken transformed me.
I was her watch to wind.

But she sauntered out as gracefully
as she sauntered in.
And now she only comes to me at night, riding a draft.
Touching nothing but that place in me that reaches.
Reaches for that which can be seen and felt but cannot
be had.

I wake to a loss heavier than all the stones
it takes to drown a poet.

Melancolony

The dark place.
The place where I understand things.
The place where I belong.
It is a country in my mind where
hope is sacrificed on an alter
to vice.

It is a melancolony.
Breathe.

I ended up here on my way to somewhere.
Somewhere.
Anywhere. Anywhere but here.
Never here!
But Melancolony pulled me in.
Breathe.

I was passing through, but I got comfortable,
lost sight of my goals,
my destination,
my truest, ascetic self.
Breathe.

I'm a settler in a dark place because I
couldn't go on,
and now I don't know how to exist
anywhere else.
Breathe.

The examples before me were irresistible.
What is a young man with nothing to mimic?
Breathe.
Here in the dark place, guilt is the language
we speak,
while we deal in sabotage of the character,
sabotage of the will.
Breathe.
I am the Melancolony saboteur.
Shame is my currency.
We strike our deals on our knees,
hands out,
palms up.
Breathe.

Forgive me father for I have sinned.
It has been nearly three hours since my
last confession.
How many Hail Mary's must I say,
till I can sin again?
Breathe.
In Melancolony,
in the blink of an eye everything can change.
Breathe.
Mountains move humans while humans change lanes.
Breathe.
Worlds collide.
Breathe.
Cells divide.
Breathe.
Combustibles combust.
Breathe.

Antiques rust.
Breathe.
And all of this while you were standing there,
in the corner,
hiding in the shadows,
back against the wall.
Breathe.
I know why eye contact is so hard for you.
People gonna do
what people gonna do.
Breathe.

They're not always gonna consult you.
Breathe.
Sometimes asinine, sometimes wise.
Breathe.
More often than not taking you by surprise.
Breathe.
Some may humiliate you, assault your quintessence
through and through.
Breathe.
They may blame you.
Try to shame you,
and claim what's yours as they "left brain" you.
Breathe.

Down here in Melancolony, we all saints.
Hospitable martyrs
in the service of the affably tyrannical.
Breathe.

You are not a loser!
Look them in the face and seethe!
And **Breathe!!**

Your tasks are impossible, and you do them anyway.
Breathe.
You're better than their best on your very worst day.
Breathe.
You're your own biggest critic and I'm your biggest fan.
Breathe.
Gonna kick your past right in the ass and grab you by the
hand.
Breathe.

We are going to walk out of Melancolony together, kicking its
dust off our shoes and raising our arms to perform obscene
gestures to a town folk with no ambition to rise above the
obscurity they revere.

Breathing in a vagabond breeze,
embracing a vagabond existence.
Wealthier with nothing and movement,
than stagnant with everything,
and blooming in Melancolony.
Breathe.

Deception Parade

I dare to write,
but I dare not speak.
I dare to look,
but I dare not seek.
I dare to walk,
but I dare not run.
I tempt the moon and
I dread the sun.

I dare to breathe,
but I dare not live.
I dare to take,
but I dare not give.
I dare to write,
but I dare not reveal.
I show you the caricature.
I hide what is real.

I'm the stained-glass window.
I'm the spoon full of sugar.
I'm the bearer of bad news.
I'm the red cape that hides the sword and
I am the sword.
I'm the cheapest whiskey,
hiding in crystal.

One day, the bull will catch on.

All the stained glass in the world
will not hide the rage.
No amount of sugar will change the taste
in his mouth.
Bad news will not stop him in his tracks.

A price must be paid.

No amount of whiskey will assuage the ancient desire for
retribution.
One day the beast will taste me.
He'll drink my blood from crystal,
or lap it off the ground.

There is one more body in the desert.
Broken.
Twisted.
Eyes vacant and staring through me.
A U-Haul trailer.

A rice -rocket.
No one could tell what kind.
We tempt our Gods.
We feed our demons.
Earth beckons flesh.

Rest easy fellow traveler.
Today, you were not alone.

The End

About The Author

Steven Prop is a 55-year-old over the road trucker. He has traveled all over the lower 48 states and Canada, and he has called home places as diverse as Bowdoinham, Maine, San Antonio, Texas and Fairbanks, Alaska.

9 798894 195674